# Life After

## *Yes*

A Christian Approach to Choosing Life,
Navigating Parenthood, and
Overcoming Poverty

Marisol Maldonado Rodriguez

Life After Yes

Copyright © 2021Marisol M. Rodriguez

RENEW Life Center

ISBN-13: 978-0-578-80869-7

# Dedication

In memory of my mom, Felicita, whose face
I see in every woman I serve.

# Table of Contents

# Acknowledgments

Writing a book is something I never dreamed I would do, and although I ultimately found it to be very rewarding, it would not have been possible without my dear friend, Sanyika Calloway, who I call my Purah.

Purah was Gideon's servant, but not just any servant. In Judges 7: 9-10, God tells Gideon to attack the camp of the Midianites and then says, "If you're afraid, take your servant Purah with you." I have to admit I know how Gideon felt. I'm often afraid of the tasks God calls me to. I think He knew that because He sent me a fearless Purah in Sanyika. She pushes me, cheers me on, and does not let me back down from a challenge. I will be forever grateful for the long days and nights of coaching, encouragement, and never-ending support. From the founding of RENEW Life Center to the writing of this book, I couldn't imagine facing these challenges without my sister in Christ, my colleague, and my friend.

I'm eternally grateful to Joan Vitale, who introduced me to pro-life ministry. I still remember the day she handed me a volunteer brochure for her pregnancy center; I remember smiling, putting the brochure in my pocket, and thinking, "Fat chance I'll ever get involved with something like that." Well, long story short, a few months later, I found myself sitting at her pregnancy center's volunteer training, and the rest is history. Joan modeled for me what it meant to be a follower and servant of Jesus Christ. I watched her week after week, and marveled at her love for Jesus, and her passion and dedication for the cause of life. I was forever changed by the years I spent serving under her leadership.

When I told my pastor, Tim Chicola, about the burden the Lord put on my heart, he said, "You should start a ministry to do that." I remember replying, "Pastor, I'm fifty years old; who starts anything at fifty?" I should've known better than to have a debate with a pastor.

He quickly shot back, "Moses got his calling at eighty." Thus, began my journey in bringing RENEW Life Center to life. Thank you for your counsel, encouragement, and support, not only in ministry but also in my personal life. I have been blessed by your spiritual leadership, and the love and support from my family at The Crossing Church. I thank you all for your generous support in making RENEW a reality; my heart is full.

When I called Lighthouse Pregnancy Resource Center to share the vision for a pregnancy center with expanded services in the city of Paterson, Executive Director Debbie Provencher answered the phone. On the other end of her line was a total stranger with nothing more than a dream. I honestly expected her to hang up on me, but instead, she heard me out because the need was clear to her as well. She invited me to share the vision with her board, and soon after, a pregnancy center "plus" was opened in Paterson, New Jersey. I am so grateful that the Lord brought our two ministries together to bring greater impact to His Kingdom. We are truly better together.

God used Armenia Liranzo to inspire a new ministry and this book. Her unplanned pregnancy, her choice for life, and her desire for a better future for herself and her baby opened my eyes to the needs of women who have taken a leap of faith to choose life. Her honesty and humility interrupted ministry as usual and led me to a broader view of what it means to be pro-life. Ten years later, I am blessed to still be a part of her life's journey, and I pray that I will be for a lifetime.

I am grateful to the women we serve at RENEW Life Center. I have learned more from them than I could ever list here. They generously shared their life stories in this book in hopes that it would ultimately help others. I admire their strength and courage to face obstacles and keep striving forward for the brighter future they want to create for their children.

During this journey, I've learned that there's the family that you birth, then there's the family that God puts together. God expanded my family when He brought Julides and her children, Angel and Jordy, into my life. You will get to know them later in this book. I am blessed by what I've learned in our journey together, and by the love we have shared among us.

My adult children, David, Marcos, Sarah, and Jon-Luke, have all used their God-given talents to serve in ministry with me. I thank them for their support in creating beautiful and delicious events for RENEW, facilitating workshops for the women we serve, years of lugging around heavy coin filled baby bottles during baby bottle fundraisers, and generously sharing their mom with others.

Finally, I want to thank my husband, Fernando, my number one supporter, and cheerleader. He always has a "word of wisdom" for me that brings questions, issues, or problems into perfect focus. I can't imagine my life's journey without him.

# Forward

ife after yes. Since saying "yes" to the role of director for a small pregnancy resource center in northern New Jersey 15 years ago, I have seen the amazing potential of the Church – with a capital "C" – to extend hope and practical help to under-resourced, overwhelmed parents. A hope and help that saves and changes lives.

Through the selfless generosity of countless individuals and churches, God has grown Lighthouse to serve more and more women and couples facing unexpected pregnancies. As we were being led to open the first pregnancy center for Paterson, our state's third largest city and one of its most challenged urban areas, God led us to Marisol Rodriguez. This divine encounter included her three equally passionate co-laborers in the founding of RENEW Life Center (Evelyn, Michele and Sanyika).

These women were familiar with the good work of pregnancy centers because they had served in them. But they also knew there was more good work that needed to be done after the precious "yes" was delivered into the arms of a courageous mom. The services of a pregnancy center typically extend through pregnancy and a child's first year of life. But the complex issues and deep needs of under-resourced parents extend back several generations – and will ripple forward to the next generations, without extensive intervention.

Marisol and the co-founders of RENEW Life had experienced generational and situational poverty in their own lives. This gave them an understanding, empathy – and a burning desire – to equip other parents in poverty to thrive as they raise the next generation.

Lighthouse and RENEW Life joined forces to address the immense challenges mothers face as they struggle to say "yes" to a new life. We suspected we would be better together, and five years later, it seems we were right. We are ALL better together. God has made us so we need each other.

If your heart is already saying, *"Yes, I want to do more for struggling parents and their children,"* you will love this book's practical applications. If you have said, "Yes," to a life of following Christ but have never considered your responsibility to parents in poverty, I ask you to read this book with an open heart. And most of all, I pray God will use you – as he has used Marisol -- to make a wonderful difference in this world.

**Debbie Provencher,**
Executive Director, Lighthouse Pregnancy Resource Center

# Chapter 1

# Is Our Pro-Life View Narrow?

*"May your choices reflect your hopes, not your fears."*

**Nelson Mandela**

As someone who served in pro-life ministry for over a decade, I never thought that my view of pro-life ministry was narrow. On November 2, 2010, that changed.

I was the Client Services Director of a pregnancy resource center located in a large city in New Jersey. I had served as a volunteer at this center for almost ten years before I took on the director's role, and during that time, I thought I had developed a pretty good understanding of the pro-life cause and the many issues surrounding it.

However, on that fateful day back in 2010, everything changed. I received an email from one of our clients. She had been abortion-minded when she visited us, but with the counsel and encouragement from one of our volunteers, she made a choice for life. Let me tell you a few things about this woman: she had a college degree, she had a full-time career path job, and she was a go-getter. So what I read in her email really rocked me to the core. Here is her message, shared with her permission:

**From:** ███████████████████████

**Date:** November 2, 2010 at 10:13:14 PM EDT

**To:** ███████████████

**Subject: please advise me**

Hello Marisol,

How have you been? I've been trying to stay close to God and do His will, but things seem not to be going as planned. I'm five months pregnant, and I'm scared. My debt-to-income ratio is so close that I'm living paycheck to paycheck, and I haven't found a way to budget getting any supplies for the baby to come. I'm not sure what I'm having (boy or girl), but I've been feeling depressed, and I've been crying a lot. I'm not sure where or who to turn to because my family has become too busy for me. I'm already stressing out due to my instability, and to add to the matter, my mom will not be able to babysit for me while I'm at work. I'm at my wit's end trying to plan and be able to survive on my check while providing for this baby that God put here for some reason. I'm very sad because when I first spoke to ████, I was walking a thin line with the decision of having this baby, and now that I've made this decision, I'm not sure what to do to continue moving forward. Is there any way you can help me? Do you know where I can get the baby supplies, breast pump stuff, furniture, babysitting services, anything (quality materials and services for a low price)? I would like the baby to have something even if I have nothing. I have a TV that sits on top of a milk crate, I'm sleeping on a bed that hurts my back, and it's mismatched; one part is full, the other a queen, the base doesn't fit, I'm grateful I'm not sleeping on the floor. I don't want to be a failure, but I'm lost. Can you help me get back on track?

**Armenia**

I was stunned. I could not wrap my head around what I just read. I could sense her pain through her words. Initially, I was angry at myself; how did I drop the ball like that? I thought that because she had an education and a career, she would be okay. I knew that pregnancy outside of marriage would put her in some difficulty, that was to be expected. But, what I didn't think about was the fear and loneliness she was feeling. Worse of all, at five months pregnant, she was beginning to regret choosing to have her baby because she felt alone in that decision.

The email broke my heart, and it got me thinking: "If this woman, who is much further ahead educationally and economically than most of my clients, was struggling so badly, what was happening to my typical client?" The thought scared me. But it was also the impetus to take a closer look at what was happening in the lives of women in poverty who choose life for their babies; the very women I had seen week after week, month after month for more than a decade, without ever having this awareness brought to light.

I came to terms with the fact that my pro-life view, that of the center I worked for – and perhaps the Church in general, was too narrow. This short-sightedness was rooted in four misconceptions:

1. **After a woman chooses life, she's going to be OK**. If I put myself in the shoes of a mother with a pregnant teenager

or young adult daughter, I know I would do whatever it took to protect the life of my grandchild and my daughter's future. But not every young woman facing an unplanned pregnancy has that type of support. A woman in poverty with a pregnant daughter could protect the life of her grandchild by encouraging her daughter to choose life, but she may not be able to help protect her daughter's future. Very often, the grandmother does not have the education or resources to do that. According to the U.S. Census Bureau, "Among children living with a mother only, 40% lived in poverty." Additional research from the National Center for Health Statistics shows that the educational level of parents, particularly unwed mothers, is a key indicator of a child's likely educational level as well as other socioeconomic outcomes that will negatively affect them over the course of their lives. Not only do these children have the disadvantage of being born to parents who have low levels of education, but because they are unmarried, the familial support structure is also greatly compromised.

2. **The pregnancy resource center is an all-encompassing solution.** It's not, and it's not meant to be. Pregnancy centers are more like triage units than long-term support. Pregnancy centers are lifesavers, and they do a great job at that. Many of them have extended their services to include parenting classes and material support in the form of diapers, wipes, formula, and other basic baby items, but typically their services end a year after the baby is born. What happens after that? How does a young mom with a limited education learn to parent a difficult

teenager? What about all the financial, emotional, and spiritual support she'll need along the way?

3. **A woman and her baby can survive on government assistance.** Besides the fact that this is not true, as Christians, is that what we want? Do we only want her and her baby to survive? To barely get by? I don't think that's what God has called us to. He has called us to abundant living, and we're called to share that abundant life with others.

Gone are the days of blanket "welfare" in which all of the individual's basic survival needs were taken care of for the duration of the child's life. However, there are partial forms of government assistance such as the **S**upplemental **N**utrition **A**ssistance **P**rogram (SNAP), formerly known as food stamps; **T**emporary **A**ssistance for **N**eedy **F**amilies (TANF), formally known as welfare; as well as **T**emporary **R**ental **A**ssistance (TRA). They are not all-encompassing programs that create some sense of stability. According to the United States Department of Agriculture (USDA), "A majority of SNAP households with children were single-mother households. Only 12% received cash benefits from TANF."

Essentially this means that close to 90% of individuals who need additional financial support do not receive it. Housing support has limitations of up to two years – if it's available at all. With rising food costs and lack of access to full-service grocery stores in poverty-riddled areas (often known as food deserts), there is much less support and opportunity for a viable lifestyle. I don't mean to suggest financial security or high levels of wealth, but a dignified quality of life, and a spirit of hope are not unreasonable minimums to be met.

4. **Only unmarried and non-Christian women are abortion vulnerable**. I have seen many couples at the center who are married or engaged and are considering abortion. Why? Because they're just not ready for a child right now, they want to buy a house first, they want to pay off their student loans or get their careers off the ground. But also, there is another reality that I know of firsthand, and that is that you can be regularly attending church and still be considering an abortion.

I believe we are correct in making a focused effort in reaching abortion-vulnerable women and saving pre-born babies' lives. To that end, concerned Christians have heavily relied on pregnancy resource centers, and there have been great success stories resulting from their diligent efforts. But our life saving efforts should not end there. When a decision for life is made, we should take a look at the big picture of that woman's life and her baby's future.

RENEW Life Center was established as an on-going support and resource for women who have said yes to life, as she faces the long journey ahead. Even more so, we have to consider the root of the problem – poverty itself – and how to alleviate it.

Living in poverty does not merely mean struggling to provide basic needs due to a lack of financial stability. It is an all-encompassing condition that affects how a person feels, how they think, how they view their own future and the future of their families, how they form relationships, how they function as parents, how they practice self-esteem, and how others view them as well.

Therefore, our educational programs, mentoring/discipleship services, and leadership training are designed to transform lives, restore hope, and encourage dignity through self-sustainability. Overcoming generational poverty leads to reduced dependence on government assistance, increased self-esteem and improved relationships.

In a conversation with RENEW co-founder Sanyika Calloway, she shared the following: "Those who have never lived in poverty don't know the hurdles, the boundaries, and the detours that having an unplanned pregnancy places on a woman in poverty. So it's easy to assume or think that once she chooses life, she's going to be okay, but she's not going to be okay because she comes from a background of poverty. She has a limited education, limited options, limited life experiences, and greatly diminished chances for change, progress, or success."

These are the women that I'm focused on. If you come from a middle-income background, and if you're a teenager or college student, who becomes pregnant, you will most likely have the support you need in order to finish your college education. Your parents will rearrange their schedules, hire babysitters, and provide financial support; they will do whatever it takes to ensure you have a stable future. But if you don't have that support system as a pregnant teenager or young adult, then high school stops, and college never begins. Instead, you enter into a cycle of hopelessness and despair where one poor choice warrants another, and you don't know the way out. Moving beyond that reality becomes the rare exception rather than the regular rule.

After that harsh but necessary wake-up call from Armenia's email, I began to look more closely at the lives of my clients. I noticed things I had never seen before, although it was obvious all along. I realized that without even knowing it, I had gotten into a pattern of seeing only the problems I expected to see, rather than seeing each new individual I met as exactly that – someone who I had never met before with their own set of struggles, fears, doubts, and worries – totally unique to them.

Perspective is a powerful thing, and once you see something with a new awareness, it's hard to unsee it. The vast majority of women who walked into my center lived in poverty. Although I had been raised in poverty in that same city, I had forgotten what it was like for my mother to raise eight children completely on her own. I felt the Lord telling me I had to remember the shame, fear, and frustration of being poor. In that remembering, the Lord broke my heart, then built me back up, and gave me an expanded calling.

## An Expanded View

I shared what God had put on my heart with several of my volunteers, who had also been raised in poverty. It was something akin to discovering you all shared a secret language or a common experience that forged an irrevocable bond. I instantly gained their support in exploring the effects of poverty on women who choose life. What followed was an incredible journey of remembering our past, investigating what causes poverty,

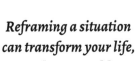

*Reframing a situation can transform your life, and your world.*

and developing a conduit through which the Church can provide ongoing support to women, children, and families in poverty.

Addressing poverty is important because we know that women in poverty are targeted for abortion. We have to understand what poverty is like for individuals and redundant families wordy better understand what they truly need to not only choose life but also to help them lead an abundant life. When we are looking at them through the lens of our middle-class lives, we assume that they have the opportunity to make the same choices we have, but that they choose something different. This is not the case. When we understand the reality of poverty, we will have a greater impact on saving lives. We will be able to see the whole picture of the woman's life, not just her unplanned pregnancy and the next few choices in front of her. We'll have an idea of what her history may have been like, and the possible course of her future. Then we can better address and quell her fears for the life in poverty she may feel trapped in.

If we care about the pro-life issue, we have to care about poverty. Period. They are inextricably linked.

According to research compiled from national studies, about 28% of single mother families were "food insecure," 12% used food pantries, and 33% spent more than one-half of their income on housing, which is generally considered the threshold for "severe housing cost burden."

Families headed by single mothers are among the poorest households. More than one-third live in poverty, and as such, are extremely vulnerable to homelessness.

Can you see now that if we separate the two, we're only doing half the job God has called us to? It's no wonder we will throw our hands up in the air in disbelief when the same girl keeps coming back pregnant again and again. The majority of unplanned pregnancies and abortions occur to women in poverty. If you want to stop or reduce unplanned pregnancies and abortions in the poverty population, you have to address poverty itself. It's not a religious issue, although Philippians 2:4 tells us, "Let each of you look not only to his own interests, but also to the interests of others." It's not a political issue, though we should vote for leaders who support our biblical view. It's an economic issue.

## Generational And Situational Poverty

I've been speaking of poverty in general terms, I would like to make some important distinctions.

There are two types of poverty: generational and situational. You're in generational poverty when you come from a background of poverty for two generations or more. That means that your parents are in poverty, and your grandparents were as well. Situational poverty is when an event, such as the loss of a job, an illness, or a divorce, throws you into poverty. It's important to note that when you're in situational poverty, it's easier to get out because you have the skills, contacts, and resources to get back on your feet with some effort and time. When you come from generational poverty, you don't have any of that. There's a huge knowledge gap that is not covered in school, not modeled by your family, not seen in the lives of those you interact with, and not understood by the individual.

Middle-income families naturally pass down to their children the skills needed to live productive and economically stable lives. In poverty, the skills that are passed down are based on survival.

That's what a woman's parents know how to do well; that's what is taught, or in most cases "caught," as in picked up through the experiences of her life.

What you see in families are cycles of greater wealth creation or cycles of greater entrenched poverty. We have the opportunity to use the unplanned pregnancies women are facing to save lives, save souls, and interrupt poverty patterns for generations to come. I love Isaiah 58 and in particular verses 6-9:

> **6** *"Is not this the kind of fasting I have chosen:*
> *to loose the chains of injustice*
> *and untie the cords of the yoke,*
> *to set the oppressed free*
> *and break every yoke?*
>
> **7** *Is it not to share your food with the hungry*
> *and to provide the poor wanderer with shelter—*
> *when you see the naked, to clothe them,*
> *and not to turn away from your own flesh and blood?*
>
> **8** *Then your light will break forth like the dawn,*
> *and your healing will quickly appear;*
> *then your righteousness will go before you,*
> *and the glory of the Lord will be your rear guard.*
>
> **9** *Then you will call, and the Lord will answer;*
> *you will cry for help, and he will say: Here am I.*

God gives us clear instructions on how we should address poverty and oppression. He then tells us why we should do it; because our well-being is tied to theirs.

## Bringing Options To Light

Often as I sat across from a woman considering an abortion, the stories they shared were the same. She had a dream. Maybe the goal was to be the first person in her family to graduate from high school or college. Perhaps it was to have a career and help her mom and siblings have better lives. She aspires to something that no one in her family has ever been able to do. She hasn't seen it role modeled. She doesn't know how to get from here to there. But what she's sure of is that this pregnancy will put an end to her dream.

At that moment, we have the opportunity to tell this woman that there's a third option. An option where she can choose life and her dreams as well. But we have to show her that it is possible. If she's willing to do the hard work of bringing a child into the world, raising it, and pursuing her goals – there are people and resources that can help her make her dream a reality and will come alongside her in solidarity and consistent support.

When we show her that we are the guardians of her dreams and shepherds of her soul, we show her that we love her, her baby, and their future. They all matter to God and to us, too.

## What A Difference One Church Can Make

I was born to a single woman in Puerto Rico who already had six children. Her life was hard. She was orphaned by the age of nine, never went to school, and other than cooking, cleaning, and raising children, she didn't have any particular work skills. She was wholly dependent on the man in her life for survival.

My father, the latest man in her life, was an abusive, violent man; but she was thankful that he kept her and her children fed, housed, and safe from *other* predators. In 1965, my father brought us all to New Jersey. Here, in one generation, the course of life for her descendants changed forever! Her children were moved from generations of abject poverty, no education, and no marriages, to educated, skilled professionals, marriages, and home owners who never spent a day on welfare once they reached adulthood.

How did she do it? She didn't. At least not on her own. She stepped into a church, and that made all the difference in our world.

My mother was introduced to the Lord in Puerto Rico by a neighbor named Doña Mery. My older sisters told me that she was a very kind older woman with long white hair in a bun. Every time Doña Mery saw my mother outside hanging laundry on the clothesline, she would come out to tell her about Jesus and invite her to church. After many of these conversations, my mother accepted her invitation and went to church with her. That day, her life and ours changed forever.

When my mother arrived in New Jersey, the first thing she did was look for a church. She found a small storefront church in Newark. It was a poor church; it didn't have many resources, and there were only a couple of middle-income families who were part of the congregation. The members were kind, and made us feel welcomed.

At that time, we lived in a tiny two-bedroom apartment. My mom converted the dining room into a third bedroom for herself and my father. The kids were crammed into the other two bedrooms. That was my life; we barely survived, but it was the same thing in every other house in our neighborhood, so I thought that was normal. What I knew wasn't normal was my father's violent and erratic behavior. I knew it, but I never spoke about it. As a matter of fact, I don't remember us talking about it at home among ourselves either. That's just the way it was, and we accepted it. We kept our heads down, mouths shut, and stayed clear of him as best we could. That was until the church got involved in my mother's life. The more they found out about what was happening in our home, the more they got involved. The women rallied around my mother with love and support. As the pastor made a plan to have my father removed from the home, others in the church taught my mother about social services and how to apply for them so that she didn't have to rely on my father for survival. Otherwise, she would have never agreed to have him removed from our home.

I was only a little girl, so the plans to have him removed weren't discussed with me, but I remember the day the plan was put in motion. Our pastor sat nervously on our couch, waiting for my father to come home from work, while two police officers were stationed outside the house in case things became violent, which it seemed most certainly that they would. I remember my mother was very scared; she was terrified of my father. But, she put her trust first in God, and then in her new family.

Although there was much fear and chaos, the plan worked. My father was removed; he got the message that my mom was not alone anymore, and she was not fair game for his rage and abuse. There was now a group of people who surrounded her and supported her. The few times he attempted to make his way back into our home, he was reminded that things had changed. A new life had begun for us. And all it took was the body of Christ to see, listen, and take action boldly. From then on, my mother and her children were finally free from the tyranny of my father.

Although she probably did not feel that way at the moment, my mother was one of the lucky ones. Raising eight children as a single mother might not sound like a dream arrangement, but she was surrounded by people determined to love, protect, and nurture her and her family. They kept away the elements that threatened to disrupt her making progress. Her blessing was in finding the church before the situation got so bad that the way out was no longer clear.

But just as important as the church's role, was my mother's desire to have a better life and her willingness to work for it even when times were tough and things seemed impossible. She was willing to accept that the way out of poverty was not by finding a man to take care of you, but rather by empowering yourself to work out of the situation and empower your children to never have to face it.

# Chapter 2

# The Consequences
# of That Narrow View

*"Wisdom consists of the anticipation of consequences."*

**Norman Cousins**

What happens when we don't take a broader view of our pro-life ministry and how that affects the work? Two things come immediately to mind.

One is that women and children needlessly suffer, and the suffering extends for generations with far-reaching social and spiritual implications for the world. The other is the sharp criticism from pro-abortion advocates who say we only care about the baby.

We care for the woman as well. When we spare a baby from abortion, we also spare a woman from a lifetime of regret and possible serious consequences to her physical and emotional well- being.

## Unplanned Pregnancies, Poverty And Abortion

I want to discuss the relationship between unplanned pregnancies, poverty, and abortion. I want us to understand the relationships between them so we can comprehensively serve the abortion-minded woman.

Early on in exploring these relationships, RENEW co-founder Sanyika Calloway came across a book titled, *"A Framework for Understanding Poverty"* by Ruby K. Payne, Ph.D. Dr. Payne is an expert on the mindsets of economic classes. Her book helped us understand our history of poverty and helped us better understand the women we serve. I reached out to Dr. Payne and asked her if I could interview her to discuss the relationship between unplanned pregnancies and poverty. A partial transcript of that interview follows.

Marisol: "With free or reduced cost contraceptives made available to people in poverty, why are there so many unplanned and unmarried pregnancies in poverty?"

Dr. Payne: "To not have a pregnancy, you have to plan, and the more unstable your environment, the more difficult it is to plan. Coupled with the fact that criminologists will tell you, they can predict the amount of violence in the neighborhood by two things: the adults' educational attainment level and the number of households who do not have men living in them permanently. This leaves women in these neighborhoods with a need for protection. If you want protection and you want a man in your household, what's going to be his incentive to stay with you? If you love that man and want to show him that you love him, you will give him a child because it's proof of his masculinity. That's not understood in the middle class at all."

Marisol: "Can you expand on the reality of women in poverty needing protection?"

Dr. Payne: "People who have never experienced poverty do not understand that if you're a female in poverty and you live in a high poverty area, you have to have protection or you are everybody's game. You're a target for everybody. And not only are you a target for everybody, but so are your children. You can't protect your children alone. They're vulnerable because, in poverty, the clear understanding is if there's no man around, you're fair game. The closer you get to survival, the more you're going to use physical approaches to survive. When the media talks about single mothers in poverty, they talk about the fact that they don't have money, sometimes they talk about the fact that they don't have time to be with their children because they're working two jobs, but it's an even deeper issue; they don't have anybody to protect them or their children.

The reality is that the protective mechanism for women in poverty oftentimes is to go to a man for protection. A lot of times, the whole discussion is about money and time. But at the heart of the matter is the fact that if you want to survive a high poverty neighborhood, protection is huge."

As I listened to Ruby talk about protection, so many conversations I have had with women at the center came into focus. The decisions my mother made around men came into focus. They weren't weak-willed women; they wanted to ensure their survival and that of their children. My mother had five daughters. Her involvement with my father, a man who was well known and feared in our area, assured her daughters' safety; we were untouchable, although it was at the expense of the abuse she had to endure.

I felt conviction over the times I had rolled my eyes and thought, "Here she is again; another man, another baby," whenever I saw a woman back at the center numerous times. All along, I was not understanding the reality of the world she lived in.

## The Hard Truth

I interviewed one of the women we serve at RENEW for this book regarding generational poverty, unplanned pregnancies, and the need women have for protection; she responded:

> When girls like myself choose life, and then find ourselves in difficult situations we lean on the wrong support – another man, for example. Then we end up pregnant again by a man who is not providing for us. How do we come back to you and say: 'Oh, you know what, Marisol, I did it again.' It's a cycle; we're looking for help, we're looking for a need to be met, so we gravitate to a man, and we cling to him.

What she shared is not lost on me, although it took a decade for me to better understand it. When we have a need, we will do whatever it takes to fill the void. That reality, along with a woman's feelings of abandonment by the absence of her own father in her life, is very real. They are drawn towards finding what looks like the chance for safety and security, even if it's only for a short while.

The ability to create a space for a woman in poverty to articulate how she is feeling has brought about some of the most emotionally powerful conversations I've ever had. For many of the women who sat across the room from me, it was the first time someone asked them what effect choosing life had on them. Once they began talking, the trickle of words and phrases turned into a raging river of thoughts and feelings. But what about the other part of this equation? What about the person whose only fault is being born into a situation where poverty is thrust upon them? They suffer in ways that they won't remember and ways that become ingrained in their identities.

Here's what BMC Psychiatry (BioMed Central), an open access, peer-reviewed journal, had to say about poverty's effect on the physical and mental health of both mother and baby.

Poverty is one of the most significant social determinants of health and mental health, intersecting with all other determinants, including education, local, social and community conditions, race/ethnicity, gender, immigration status, health and access to health care, neighborhood factors, and the built environment (e.g., homes, buildings, streets, parks infrastructure). The mental health effects of poverty are wide-ranging and reach across the lifespan.

Individuals who experience poverty, particularly early in life or for an extended period, are at risk of a host of adverse health and developmental outcomes throughout their life. Poverty in childhood is associated with lower school achievement; worse cognitive, behavioral, and attention-related outcomes; higher rates of delinquency, depressive and anxiety disorders; and higher rates of almost every psychiatric disorder in adulthood. Poverty in adulthood is linked to depressive disorders, anxiety disorders, psychological distress, and suicide.

If you can imagine the feeling of being stuck in quicksand and struggling to get out, you can imagine what it feels like to live in poverty. Every slight movement to escape is met with the equal possibility of being sucked further down if you fail. Now imagine a child in that same scenario, born into it without even realizing the danger they face from day one, never grasping that their normal isn't what life should look like.

## Neighborhood Deprivation And Breaking The Cycle

Findings indicate that geographically concentrated poverty, often in urban areas, is particularly toxic to psychiatric well-being. Signs of social and physical disorder often characterize poor neighborhoods, which can cause stress, undermine health-promoting social ties, and affect the mental health of people who live there.

Neighborhood deprivation has been associated with many of the same mental health outcomes as poverty, even while controlling for individual poverty. Institutional and structural mediators include the quality of local services and schools, as well as the physical distance between residents and social isolation. Community-level mediators include collective efficacy, socialization by adults, peer influences, social networks, exposure to crime and violence, and safety fears. Individual-level poverty moderates the relationship between neighborhood deprivation and mental health, with poorer families affected more adversely by area-level poverty.

Another point to note is that a 2017 report from the Urban Institute stated that only 62% of children in poverty get a high school diploma by the age of 20. These children often start life at a disadvantage that makes achievements later in life more difficult.

To break the cycle of poor education, physical and mental health issues perpetuated by poverty, we need to take a comprehensive approach that addresses all the issues. Through referrals to social services, deep meaningful relationships, and discipleship, we can work collaboratively with families in a strengths-based manner to improve the future of mother and child.

In Chapter One, I mentioned that pregnancy resource centers are like medical triage units; their job is to stop the "bleeding" and get the client "resuscitated." When it comes to the quality of life for the mother and child, this must become the job of the Church. I can attest to this in my own life, and that of my mother. Without the hands-on support of committed and caring believers, we would have been without the vital life support we needed.

I once counseled an eighteen-year-old woman to choose life. Fifteen years later, she came back with her daughter, hoping that she would also choose life. I'm glad she remembered us and came back, but that's one instance where we know that transformation didn't happen. That woman's life was not transformed to the point she could teach her children better or that she could now model things differently. That new generation received the same modeling and messaging from the older generation.

## Unplanned Pregnancies And Poverty

Single motherhood is hard, and as I have stated, it often leads to poverty and fewer opportunities, but it's even more so for teen moms. According to a study from the National Conference of State Legislatures (NCSL), teen pregnancy is strongly linked to poverty. Some 63% of teen mothers receive public assistance within the first year of a child's birth; and 52% of mothers on welfare had their first child in their teens.

Teen mothers are less likely to complete high school or college and are therefore less likely to find well-paying jobs. The economic consequences of dropping out of high school contribute to the perpetual cycle of economic hardship and poverty that can span generations.

To make matters worse, child support – which generally represents a vital income source for single mothers – is usually not in play due to the fact that young fathers often have limited educational attainment and earning potential as well.

We must recognize that crime, poverty, violence, abuse, and lack of stable and healthy family relationships are only some of the factors that can lead children to join gangs, or turn to prostitution, stripping, and other morally corrupt, short-term solutions for income. If a child is growing up without a father, and their mother has no social support, no community, no healthy male presence to fill the father's role, then we shouldn't be surprised when he or she becomes involved in behaviors that will create a sense of belonging and safety, even if it's at the expense of their personal freedom and dignity. There's a big empty hole that is left to be filled, and that hole should be filled by the Church. If we don't take the initiative, someone or something else will. The possibility of that "someone" or "something" being as positive and fruitful as the Church, given the circumstances, is close to zero.

## Am I My Brother's Keeper?

The answer is a resounding yes! We have to actively show our care and commitment to their well-being, whether it's a woman with a child in her womb or sixteen years later when the child is going through a difficult stage. Where can we show up to demonstrate that? What is our responsibility as Christ-followers – not only on the front lines of the pro-life issue but also in our communities? How can we as pro-life people seek justice for people of all ages and life situations?

> *Poverty is not just an economic disadvantage, it's a life of vulnerability and hopelessness.*

We must recognize that poverty is not just an economic disadvantage; it's a life of vulnerability and hopelessness. Single mothers are at high risk for poor mental and physical health, along with a sense of despair and helplessness, all of which are passed to their children. Youth living in impoverished neighborhoods are at risk of becoming hopeless about their future and engaging in violent behavior. When you have no future to look forward to, and when your role models are the gang members and drug dealers on the street, how can you be expected to live differently without having different role models, different tools, and a different reality to aspire to? We have to help these youth hope against hope, to help them believe that a life beyond that which is played out in their day-to-day lives is possible.

## No God - No Hope

Hopelessness comes primarily from not knowing God. Those of us who know Christ know that we find hope in all situations. Now imagine not having that hope in Christ, living in an economically depressed area where everything around you is bleak and dark. Hope cannot be produced out of thin air. Something has to initiate hope, and I believe to initiate hope, we have to introduce them to Christ. But then we have to bolster that belief with tangible support that they can see, hear, and touch. The Church must move from something we do once a week to a lifestyle we live out every day of the week. Darkness and despair are ever-present when we don't know God, so we must surround these families with believers who are the "hands and feet" of Jesus in a world that is hurting and crying out for help.

When you bring hope to a mom, you bring hope to her child, because she will pass it down to her children. There's a wonderful quote that I heard once: "Your ceiling becomes your children's floor." As someone who comes from poverty, I get that. I started out educationally, economically, and spiritually at the highest level my mom had attained. Unfortunately for me, that was pretty low, but it would have been a lot worse without the Church. The early involvement of the Church in my family's life made it possible for me to raise my ceiling so that my children would never experience poverty or its devastating effects the way that I had.

I am passionate about helping moms believe that they can raise their ceilings so that their children – the children we encouraged them to bring into the world, are not starting from where they did. They're starting from a different place, an elevated place, a place where the light can shine through. Leading people to hope is hard; helping them keep hope alive is even harder. Hope evaporates the moment a mom hears gunshots outside her window or smells marijuana in the hallway. It takes an ongoing relationship to lead a mom to the source of hope, and to keep reminding her that her hope is in Christ, and not her environment.

# Why Don't They Just...

Another result of our narrow view is that we don't understand the lack of opportunities a single mom experiences. We think that she knows how to get a job. That she can find childcare, or that she can go back to school. We're talking about families who don't even have Internet access or a computer in the house! She can't do distance learning; she can't do college online. Those are things that a lot of us assume are possible. When we don't understand this absence of opportunities and resources, we say things like, "Why doesn't she just leave him?" If she leaves him, who will protect her and her children in their dangerous neighborhood? In our world we don't have to think about that. Why doesn't she just get a job? Well, when your mother never had a job, and your grandmother never had a job, what does getting a job look like? How do you write a resume? How do you fill out a job application? How do you handle a job interview and the stress that comes from being in an environment and situation you were never taught to navigate?

Recognizing these obstacles, doesn't mean it's easy to address them. Not everyone that we meet at the pregnancy center who says yes to life is going to want the mentoring support and discipleship that we're offering them. But some will say yes, and those are the ones we have to focus on. We have to invest time and resources in the moms and dads who are craving community, who are craving relationships, and who are desperate for someone to demonstrate that they will walk alongside them for the long haul. Our message must be: "I am not a temporary person in your life. I am here for however long you allow..." We're asking them to make a long-term commitment by choosing life, and I'm asking the Church to make a long-term commitment, too. Through mutually respectful conversation, we, the Church, can communicate a plan to make things better.

## On The Frontlines For Life

Anna, a sidewalk counselor, spends a couple of days a week standing outside an abortion clinic hoping to talk to the women who are about to enter the clinic. It's a tough job. In my opinion, it's the toughest job in pro-life ministry. She's out there day after day, most times alone. But she's driven by the passion of giving a woman one last chance to reconsider her decision. It's a great day when a woman stops and listens to her message of life.

It also gives her the opportunity to hear the woman's story and what led her to the abortion clinic in the first place. Anna tells me it's almost always the same story: "I don't have a job," "I'm about to get evicted." "I can barely survive myself. How am I going to afford a baby?" The list of needs goes on and on. It makes sense because we know that the top two reasons women give for choosing an abortion are financial reasons. Anna says, "I can't say, "Hey, I know it's tough, but you should have the baby anyway. Abortion is a sin."

"I have to offer her real tangible help. I have to say: "We care about you and the baby; there is help available for you to get on your feet; you are not in this alone." That's what gets a woman to turn away from the abortion clinic."

Tom is a young man who recently started joining Anna on the sidewalk of the abortion clinic. He's hoping to talk to the men who are accompanying the women to the clinic. Early on, he gets his first save! Tom is super excited that God used him in this way. He spoke to a man named Alex, who was walking into the abortion clinic with his girlfriend, Priscilla. Tom told Alex about the developmental stage of the baby, which meant there was a beating heart. Alex tells Tom that his hours have been cut at work; he's trying to find more work but hasn't had any luck. Priscilla is also out of work because of the at-risk pregnancy, and her need to be off her feet. The basement apartment they have been living in turns out to be an illegal rental. The owner of the house has been fined, and now they have to move out within sixty days. They have nowhere to go and no money.

These problems grow out of the brokenness of our culture. We have to answer their real needs with tangible assistance. So, Tom said what he thought he should say: "We care about you and the baby. There is help available for you to get on your feet, we can help you find a place to live. You are not in this alone." Tom offers to take them to the local pregnancy center, and in that instant, Alex tells his girlfriend, Priscilla, "Let's go with him." What stood out to me when I heard this story, was how quickly this couple trusted a total stranger's offer to help; it leads me to believe that they really didn't want an abortion. They grasped the first and only offer for help they received. They just couldn't see how they would get out of the mess on their own.

It was exciting that Tom made his first abortion clinic save, but he was about to face a problem that he didn't see coming. When he promised that "we" would help them get on their feet and find a place to live, who exactly is the "we"? Was he referring to government social services? If he was, they may be on a waiting list for years. Was he referring to the pregnancy center?

Pregnancy resource centers provide a wide range of support and services and may refer them to resources or shelters. But, generally speaking, pregnancy centers are not in the housing business, and that's okay because that's not their primary mission.

When Tom spoke to Anna about the need Alex and Priscilla had, he quickly found out that "we" was a huge vacuum. That vacuum, which I became aware of through Armenia's email, is the reason I wrote this book. When Tom made the bold proclamation of additional support, he was confident that he was just the first runner of a lifesaving relay team. He assumed that every leg of the journey had someone with open arms and resources that would do everything possible to help Alex and Priscilla.

He would pass the baton to the next runner, the pregnancy center, and the needs of this couple and countless others like them would be met. All he has to do is go back to the abortion clinic and try to rescue the next baby; his job is done. The pregnancy center does its work and then passes the baton to the Church. The Church is the final runner of this race. It's where the finish line is crossed, and lives are not just saved but transformed through Jesus Christ. It's seldom that easy, even with so many people fully committed to the cause. There are many questions to be answered. Which church? How do they go about it? How is it organized?

## Relay Race For Life

To try and frame those answers in a better light, I took them to my pastor, Tim Chicola, Senior Pastor of The Crossing Church in Livingston, New Jersey, who answered these tough questions with compassion and honesty.

**Marisol:** What do you see as the role of the Church in helping women and men choose life?

**Pastor Tim:** "It is incumbent upon the Church to teach that we have to preserve life, and especially when we're talking about life in the womb. If we don't protect it, then we are really part of the problem. In a sense, we are more of a tool of Satan than anything else. If we're silent, we're a tool of the evil one. If we're too busy, we're a tool of the evil one. If we say that we desire to see Christ formed in people, then we have to be supportive of life and supportive of women who choose life. I think it's a foundational issue.

**Marisol:** You said that the Church should support the women who choose life, but how?

**Pastor Tim:** I think there has to be education. Depending on a woman's upbringing, she may not have received the education she needs to create a healthy and stable home life for herself and her baby. And she also needs Biblical teaching.

Beyond education, we have to get our hands dirty, as Jesus did. Sure, He sent the 12 apostles out two by two, but when they went out to do ministry, it was a ministry that He was already doing. When He sent them out, it was not to do something they had never seen before. We need to get in there, so to speak, and one by one, rescue these women educationally, spiritually, emotionally, and physically. After the birth, that's when the work really has to begin, and unfortunately, a lot of times, the Church doesn't know how or where to help.

When I was younger, I remember going to abortion clinics and standing in front, telling women, "Don't get an abortion." If you were ever successful, you go Hallelujah, high five, and then that was it. I went home, and that was the end of everything. But it was just the beginning for this woman and child. The challenge that these women face many times, especially if they've been in a crisis pregnancy situation, is that sometimes they don't have strong support at home; they don't have emotional support, spiritual support, or financial support. Lots of times, when they decide to do what is right – to preserve the image of God – their troubles just begin.

Like the good Samaritan story, the Samaritan saw a man who was beaten up and was in need, so he helped. If those who are sensitive to the Spirit of God know that there is a need and have the wherewithal to help, if we don't help, then for me, it is a sin.

Now that does not mean we can cure all the world's ills, but we are called as Christians not only to preach the gospel and set the captives free, set hearts free, unshackle them, but to also work for the betterment of culture, society, and injustice. We are called to participate in those things that make life better here on earth. The gospel calls me to love the Lord God with all my heart and all my strength and to love my neighbors as myself. So even if someone is not a Christ-follower, I am called to help him or her as I am able. I think the Church has long been weak in the post-decision-making process that a woman enters into often alone. God forbid that we continue to do that anymore. I think we've seen enough; we know enough, and I think it's time to participate in the critical areas of feeding, housing, clothing, and finding jobs."

**Marisol:** You mentioned that you felt the Church has been weak in the area of support after the "yes." Can you tell me how the Church can improve on that?

**Pastor Tim:** "I don't think we have a choice but to expand our involvement in the areas I mentioned; feeding, housing, clothing, and finding jobs; often, churches don't know how to go about doing that. That's the reason why we got excited when presented with the prospect of becoming involved with RENEW Life Center. We know that once a woman says yes, her problems multiply. But we didn't know how to help, except in a very shotgun approach. When you presented us with a thoughtful, comprehensive approach to support women after they say yes to life, that was a very exciting prospect. I'll never forget what you said; it got me to say, 'OK, I need to hear more about this.'

"You responded, "We want to help move women out of generational poverty and into self-sustainability."

"Now, for some reason, of all the things you said, that stood out to me, it struck me that, aside from all the spiritual dimension of things that we want women to embrace, that we talk about all the time in church, that we could also play a part in taking a woman who is dependent and help usher her into independence, but what was exciting and astonishing to me was to take part in something that would actually have somebody become a contributor to her community, a taxpayer.

"So, to be able to see someone make a fair wage, to be able to raise their children well, to be able to pay for their housing, to me was exciting, and that's what excited our elders too. They get it. When people move out of poverty, society is better, and their children's outcomes will be better.

"One of the loudest criticisms the pro-life movement receives from pro-abortion advocates is that we only care about the baby.

Our response has to be a tangible one that wraps its arms around the entire situation and offers practical help and hope.

"All around us, there are barriers and walls that have come up. The brilliant thing about RENEW Life Center is that you break down those barriers and walls so that people are now open to other things you want to address. But let's say you help somebody get on the right path economically, and for whatever reason, they reject the profoundly spiritual things.

"Still, you have been the hands and feet of Jesus Christ. Jesus healed people. Did all of them end up being disciples? Absolutely not. But He healed those who could not walk, could not speak, or who were possessed. Was it a good thing? Was society helped? Were families strengthened?

"Absolutely, just by the kind acts and the healings that were done. So, RENEW Life Center, in many ways, is a healing center; that's how we've always looked at it. By supporting RENEW Life Center financially and through the volunteer efforts of our congregation, I believe we have taken a step in the right direction in helping women who have chosen life."

## The Clock Is Ticking

Because of the gap in support, instead of going back to his life-saving work, Tom now finds himself scrambling, trying to find a way to keep his promise of support to this couple. The couple only has sixty days to move, and the clock is ticking. Tom and Alex have been in communication. Alex tells him that everywhere he goes, they're asking him for large sums of money to secure an apartment. They would be happy just to rent a studio or a room, but that's not working out either. Tom can sense the stress in his voice. Tom asks Anna for financial help for this couple, and she responds generously. He goes across the street from the abortion clinic, where Christians often gather to pray, and he asks them for help. They're surprised that he has to do this. They also thought that those kinds of needs were being taken care of by the pregnancy center. When they find out that it's not that simple, they all gladly give.

Thank God Tom was able to gather enough money to help Alex and Priscilla secure a deposit for an apartment, but it took weeks to gather the money, weeks that could've been spent in front of the clinic saving other lives. Besides, how many times can he go back to the same people to ask for help? The handoff of the baton isn't a smooth one. There is often no one on the other end to pick up the necessary slack that is a real reality of bringing a child into the world and navigating the challenges of poverty and lack of resources.

At the time I'm writing this, the couple is about to move into their apartment. Alex's employer moved him back to full-time status, he has secured a second job, and Priscilla is due in a few weeks. There will definitely be other hurdles ahead, like obtaining childcare so Priscilla can work. RENEW is working with this couple to help them build an emotionally healthy and economically stable home for their baby to grow. Our hope is that we'll find Christian mentors who will model a healthy marriage relationship, lead them to a relationship with Jesus Christ, and travel the journey of life alongside them.

# Chapter 3

# Nine Months to Life

*"If motherhood is a labor of love, then single motherhood requires double the labor and double the love."*

**Unknown**

For some women, receiving the news that they are pregnant feels like a life sentence.

Co-founder Sanyika Calloway reflects on her unplanned pregnancy at the age of sixteen: "Depending on your perspective, you can think this is awesome. I am carrying a life. I am bringing a new life into this world. But for me, it was a life sentence that quite literally felt like an albatross. It was a weight that I did not want to carry. I could not see a future. I could not see completing high school. I could not see leaving the small town that I grew up in. I could not see college. I could not see a life that was full and felt fulfilled as a single mother. So, I chose to have an abortion. For me, it seemed like the only way out of the prison I already felt trapped in."

Saying yes to life shouldn't be a life sentence to poverty, hopelessness, and despair, but that's exactly how it feels for many women. And unless there's an intervention, that's exactly what it can become.

It does not just feel that way for single women in poverty; it can also feel like a life sentence for a married, middle-class woman in a verbally abusive relationship.

In 1993, I was married and had two beautiful sons, a four-year-old and a two-year-old. My marriage was a difficult one; it was filled with delusional jealousy, verbal, and emotional abuse. I'm not the type of woman to tolerate this for long, so I suggested marriage counseling, my husband refused. He was from a different culture, and he didn't see anything wrong with his behavior.

"I realized things were not going to change, but I couldn't just ask for a divorce. He was originally from another country, and I feared he would take my boys abroad, and I would not be able to get them back, so I made an escape plan. I opened a bank account, and without him knowing, I slowly started to funnel money into it. I was able to accumulate ten thousand dollars in that account, and my plan was to take the money and my boys and move to a part of the country where the cost of living was more affordable.

I would have money to start off with while I was looking for a job, and I was confident I would not have a problem getting a job. I had built up a significant skill set in the years I spent in the Information Technology (IT) field. I had money, I knew where I was going, and I had contacts there who would support me. All systems were go! Or so it seemed.

That was until I realized my period was late. I anxiously took a home pregnancy test, and it came back positive. I felt my world turn black. I felt sick and angry. Self-hatred bubbled up inside of me and gripped my throat as if it were choking me. But mostly, I felt trapped. My mind was racing, and the only solution I could think of was to kill myself. I wanted out of this situation, this marriage, this life, and I wanted out now! How would I do it? When?

Thankfully I looked to my left and saw my boys sleeping. I couldn't do that to them. They would grow up thinking that their mother was a coward, and she left them to be raised by a father who would teach them to be just like him. I could stand the thought of that even less than the thought of staying in this marriage. So suicide was not an option, but I was still trapped. I needed a Plan B, and that was an abortion. I grew up in the Church, and I was attending church. I knew it was a sin, I knew it was murder, but I also knew that both of us could not survive. It was either me or it – this unborn child who was the only thing standing between me and my freedom.

For the next few days, there was a battle inside of me. "You can't do that; it's murder, a sin!" followed up by "But you'll die, your plan will die, your hope for a new life will die!" All I saw was death. It was either me and my hope for a life of peace, or the baby inside of me. One of those things had to go, I couldn't see both things surviving. I was in so much anguish that my words wouldn't do justice describing it. But if you've felt it, you know very well what I mean.

A few days later I told my mom I had to run some errands and asked her to watch the boys. When I dropped them off, she asked me if I would go to the bodega on the corner and pick up some ingredients she needed to make dinner. On the walk back from the store, I tripped on the raised sidewalk and went sliding face-first on the concrete. My hands and knees were a bloody mess. I limped back home and broke down in tears.

My mom thought I was crying about the fall, but I was crying because I was about to make a huge mistake by having an abortion, and I felt God had stopped me. Eight months later, I still felt trapped, but as I held my daughter in my arms, I felt joy for the gift God had given me. Life truly is precious. But I also felt shame that I would've chosen my life over hers. I looked at her beautiful face, and I thought that I couldn't let her grow up in the chaos I lived in. What kind of role model would I be? I was a shell of my true self as a woman. I had to figure another way out.

## Ready For A New Normal

Often, an abortion-minded woman would melt into tears when I asked about her future. I have been guilty of thinking, "Come on, don't be selfish! You can make an adoption plan. In nine months, the baby will be born, and you can go on as normal." But what if she doesn't want to go on as normal – what if she wants something different? When my daughter was born, I didn't want to go back to normal either, but I also had the resources and support to make a change. The woman sitting in a pregnancy center often doesn't.

I've heard my clients say, "I don't want to be a statistic." They know the statistics. They know that they're becoming a part of those dreaded numbers, and they don't want that, because it brings shame, guilt, and self-hatred. They're becoming the very thing they never wanted to be.

In a subsequent conversation I had with Armenia, the young woman who sent me the email seeking help, she said, "I had expectations for my life when I found myself in this pregnancy situation. But I thought everything was going to work out because I was with this good guy. But then my family falls apart, my mom, my boyfriend, everybody. I found myself getting bits and pieces of furniture donated from people or stuff left on the curb. So literally, the stuff I had, I had gathered. I was thinking, I'm a gatherer now. I was trying to do my best, but I was not making it. How can I bring a child into the world when I can't even provide for myself? I felt lost.

"I was hearing people say that a baby was a lovely gift from God, that pregnancy was a magical experience, but it didn't feel that way for me. I felt like a burden, a beggar. I was dependent on people to survive. I felt like pregnant garbage, that was a rough time in my life."

It was painful for me to hear that; it broke me. I can't imagine what it was like to feel that way.

Unfortunately, her perspective is not uncommon for women who cannot see themselves beyond a reality that feels harsh and heavy, and that they alone have to experience.

I remember walking home from school as a teenager and looking around at my neighborhood. It was unattractive and bleak. I had this moment where I thought, "Is this what I want for my life? Is this all there is for me?" Because I had friends that lived in middle-class families, I saw that people could do better, and I decided I wanted better. Although I never faced a teen pregnancy, I didn't know how to get from where I was to where I wanted to be. No one in my family had done it before.

Fortunately for me, there were people in my church who had a vested interest in my future. Shortly after graduating high school, one of the men at the church asked me, "Marisol, what are you going to do with your life?"

Honestly, I didn't know I had a choice. When you come from generational poverty, life just happens to you; there's no planning, no dreaming, you just live and roll with the punches. I answered, "Well, I'm working at Rite Aid, but other than that, I don't know." The thought that there was a life beyond that was foreign to me. Many women I encounter at RENEW feel the same way.

## It Takes A Village, Right?

Pregnancy centers do a great job at providing support from conception throughout the nine months of pregnancy and often through the baby's first year. But upon reflection, those of us who have had children can look back at our first year of parenting and realize that that was the easy part.

Fortunately for me, I remarried an amazing man who took my children as his own. I can't imagine raising my children without my husband's support and that of my mother and sister Millie. You might be thinking: Don't the women you serve have mothers or sisters? Probably, yes, but in generational poverty, your support system isn't consistent or reliable. Everyone is busy doing what they have to do to survive. In my conversation with Dr. Payne, she frequently mentioned how poverty's instability makes it nearly impossible to plan. If we don't offer a new mom consistent and reliable support, we're asking her to take this life journey alone.

Here is what Armenia had to say about needing support:

"Now I understand the saying 'It takes a village to raise a child.' I often wish I had someone to watch the kids so I can study. Or someone to watch the kids so I can have a couple of hours to recharge before I have to begin another busy week. When I chose to carry my pregnancy to term, I didn't know what I was getting into; I didn't know all the worry and struggle I would go through. What made things worse was that I didn't have anyone to guide me."

Armenia's children are now elementary school-aged, and she doesn't know what challenges may await her during their teen years. When I think back to my children's teenage years, I'm grateful I had a husband to help with parenting, a church family that prayed for them, and a youth group that provided safe, wholesome, fun, and godly role models. I can't imagine what my children's outcome, or my sanity would have been like without that support system. Yet, we're unintentionally asking women like Armenia to go it alone. She would have to navigate the peaks and valleys of parenting on her own. Depending on how she was parented, the results can be heartbreaking.

Parenting is essential during the critical developmental years of early and middle childhood. We want to help moms stay engaged as parents, so children are not raised by the TV, the Internet, or their video games. We want to help parents gain the skills they need to feel confident in their role as they raise and discipline their children.

## Why Is Early And Middle Childhood Important?

As we delve deeper into the world that poverty creates, it is important to define what we are looking at and how it affects the children born into it. The website for the Office of Disease Prevention and Health Promotion breaks down the different phases of childhood to give us a strong grasp of the pivotal impact that early childhood can have on people.

Early childhood, defined as the period from birth until the child's eighth year of life, and middle childhood, typically the ages of 6-12, are times of enormous change in a child's life. In those formative years, children will be exposed to an enormous amount of change, new experiences, new ideas, and new environments. They will build the foundation of their social/emotional abilities, and how those translate into their physical and emotional well-being, along with how well they learn and how much value they place on their own health. Likewise, their physical and cognitive skills will be forged. The research into these areas and the policies that are brought into force are letting us know just how vital these times are in the life of a child, and who he or she will one day become.

A further breakdown shows that **early childhood** is defined by giant leaps forward in language development, socio-emotional skills, cognitive reasoning, and physical manipulation and ability.

While physical growth continues in **middle childhood**, the more profound change in the development of skills will define how well they interact socially with others. As they change from children to young adults, they begin to take on other roles and relationships that will prepare them for a productive life as an adult.

Research is conclusive that our experiences from these first two stages of childhood, for good or bad, will shape a lot of what we are able to do over a lifetime, particularly when it comes to development and learning, not just in school but over the course of a lifetime. A child's ability to be ready for school and thus ready for life as a successful contributing member of society down the line, is in direct correlation to how their early experiences are prepared for and handled.

Failure to provide a healthy environment can cause long-term damage in the form of early development of pre-disease pathways. Childhood is particularly critical to brain development, as the human brain grows to some 90% of its full size by the age of three. In this early stage of life, not only are we learning to problem-solve and communicate, and how to move about, but the bedrock of our emotions – things like trust, kindness, love – are formed, along with their polar opposite.

Negative factors, be it poor care, unsafe living conditions, burdening children with expectations beyond their ability, etc., can severely delay or damage healthy development. The damage is not temporary, either. Imagine a skyscraper with cracks in the foundation. Building another fifty stories on top of it isn't going to make it any stronger. Eventually, it will have problems that will become severely damaging to the structure as a whole.

Positive role models and caregivers, along with a safe environment and emotional support at this age, translate into the best chance for any person to live their best life through forming skills that lead to academic success, the ability to self-discipline, good eating habits, risk avoidance, an understanding of what good health looks like, the ability to form healthy relationships and solve interpersonal disagreements.

All of these vital needs come together during the first decade or so of a child's life. And yet, single mothers seldom have any support in ensuring those needs are met. More often than not, a single mother has to pay someone else – a daycare center or a sitter – to ensure her children are fed and taken care of, during the long hours she works to make ends meet. A mom struggles with keeping herself upbeat and determined; having the energy to provide developmental support to her children can seem overwhelming and is often instead addressed with the path of least resistance.

## Parenthood Is Permanent

As pro-life advocates, we are inviting young men and women into the permanent reality of parenthood. There is no divorce, and there is no breaking it off. Now, of course, there are unfortunate realities like abandonment and rejection, but perhaps with intervention, better choices could be made, perhaps these parenting relationships could have a better outcome.

As we ask women to make the permanent choice for life and parenthood, we invite you, the Christian community to come alongside them and commit to being a part of the parenting journey, to be part of the process from poverty to stability, to help usher both mother and child into a life that is abundant and hope filled.

*Poverty blocks the way for parents to perform their parental duties with full attention.*

Additionally, we want to encourage co-parenting, and when possible, marriage. Yet, without the proper preparation, counsel, and support, a marriage will not provide the physical, emotional and financial safety it was designed to bring to families. For example: A single mom has a boyfriend who is her baby's father. He's a great guy, but they do not live together. Instead, she collects food stamps, gets medical insurance, and a rent subsidy from the government.

As Christians, our natural inclination is to think that these two should be married and live as a family. I believe marriage would be a wonderful God-honoring step for this young couple, but without the preparation and support previously mentioned, the results can be less than ideal. Imagine that he is an unskilled laborer making $15/hour. He might bring home $1,800 per month after taxes. That cannot support a family.

Almost all of his income would go to pay the rent. What's left for food and utilities? Perhaps she can get a job as well, however they would have to pay for childcare and their combined income would push them above the income restriction limit to get significant government aid. So, what's the solution? We are. The Church was meant to bridge the gap. Step up and step in where support – spiritual, financial, physical – is needed.

We get involved in their lives; we role model what godly marriage and parenting look like. We nurture these young tender relationships that could blossom into marriage. We use our professional networks and personal connections to help them gain apprenticeships or internships where they build valuable work skills that can lead to economic stability so they can actually care for their families and live dignified lives.

## Stand By Me

During a conversation with her mentor, Darlene, a mother of three, mentioned that her daughter didn't want to go to school, and was giving her a hard time. Darlene was frustrated. The mentor suggested, "Why don't you talk to the teacher about it?" Darlene didn't see any point in doing that. "Nothing would change anyway", she said.

When the mentor saw her resistance, she asked some questions, and realized that the thought of meeting with a teacher was very intimidating to Darlene, especially as someone who didn't have a high school diploma. The mentor explained to Darlene the importance of being an advocate for her children. She also pointed out that if she didn't intervene now, things could get a lot worse.

The mentor told her that if she was willing, she would be happy to coach her on addressing her concerns with the teacher. It would give her the opportunity to frame her concerns in a direct and respectful format. They could also develop some questions she could ask the teacher about solving the issue. Darlene hesitantly agreed. After the coaching and practicing, Darlene was ready to make the appointment to speak to the teacher, but she made a request for her mentor to accompany her to the meeting.

When the appointment date came around, Darlene's mentor accompanied her, but she didn't say a word to the teacher. Darlene did all the talking, and she did a great job! The teacher was grateful that Darlene made her aware of her daughter's issues in class, and they quickly developed a plan to fix them. Darlene left the meeting and was ecstatic!

"Thank you! Thank you! Thank you!" she said to her mentor as she gave her a big hug. That experience empowered Darlene. It gave her confidence and pride that she could advocate for her children and make things better. Now, whenever it's necessary, Darlene calls the school, schedules appointments, addresses her concerns, and gets results all on her own. She just needed someone to show her how to do that, and to be present for support for the first time.

Mentoring can make it possible for parents like Darlene to become actively engaged in parenting and feel energized to continue the difficult task of raising children alone and in poverty.

# Chapter 4

# Approaching the Pro-Life Movement Through the Lens of the Gospel

*"Transformed people transform people."*

**Richard Rohr**

What does approaching the pro-life movement through the lens of the gospel mean to you? For me, it means to save *and* transform lives.

RENEW Life Center was founded in 2013. I thought the Lord was leading me to open a different kind of pregnancy center, one that would invite the Church into greater partnership with the center through discipleship. But wasn't it just like God to show me I wasn't dreaming nearly big enough? The three other women I co-founded RENEW with wanted the center to be in an urban area, so we searched for a city that didn't currently have one, and God led us to Paterson, New Jersey. Paterson is the third-largest city in New Jersey; it has a poverty rate of 29% compared to a rate of 10.7% across the state.

Paterson also has an alarming rate of 65% of births to unwed women, which sounded like a great place for a pregnancy center.

I decided to call the next closest pregnancy center, which happened to be only four miles away, but it was a world apart from the heart of where I sensed a real need was. I wanted to introduce myself and let them know what our plans were. The executive director invited us to meet with her and her board. At the meeting, we shared our vision of a center that provided services and support for longer than the one year after birth, that centers typically provided. Within days of the meeting, we received a call that Lighthouse Pregnancy Resource Center wanted to partner with us in making this vision a reality.

We call our collaboration *Paterson Partners for Life*; Lighthouse offers the medical services, peer counseling and parenting support and RENEW provides educational programs and services as well as long-term developmental support through discipleship and mentoring administered by church volunteers. In hindsight, I'm so grateful that the Lord brought the two organizations together to divide the heavy load of serving women, families, and communities. No one organization can do it alone. It requires the collaboration of the Church body to serve as God's hands and feet.

That same year, the two organizations, RENEW Life Center and Lighthouse Pregnancy Resource Center attended the national Care Net Pregnancy Center Conference together. Roland C. Warren had recently become the new President and CEO of Care Net, and in his keynote address, he shared the direction he saw pregnancy centers heading in. He called the vision he presented, *pro-abundant life*, and it was perfectly aligned with the collaboration RENEW and Lighthouse had begun.

When I was prompted to write this book, I knew Roland Warren was a person I wanted to interview. During our conversation he shared his pro-abundant life message:

> If you're just pro-life, then you can be an atheist and be pro-life, but you can't be an atheist and be pro-abundant life, because if you're an atheist, you're just solving for heartbeats. But if you're pro abundant life, you're solving for heartbeats that are heaven-bound.
>
> There's an extension beyond that. If a client comes in facing an unplanned pregnancy, and she brings that child into the world, that child has life, but that life is not superior in quantity and quality. You as a Christian are going to say, 'Well, that's good, but there's something that's lacking.' And that lacking piece is the abundant part of life, as opposed to just life. Jesus wasn't just pro-life. He was pro-abundant life. He said, 'I came that they might have life and that they might have it more abundantly.' In other words, I'm pro-abundant life. As a Christian, you can't be just pro-life; you actually have to be pro-abundant life. Because that's what Jesus was.
>
> That leads to why pregnancy centers can't fulfill the full pro-abundant life mission on their own. The pregnancy center can help with evangelism, but the pro-abundant life perspective is not just evangelism. It's also about discipleship.

Through relationships, we can help women and their partners transform how they view marriage and family life and guide them in making godly decisions that bring about a positive impact on their spiritual and earthly future. Thinking about it that way leads you to more of a discipleship model, which is where the Church comes in. The Church has the opportunity to use the pregnancy that a woman is facing as missionary work; it's a mission field.

It's like if the woman at the well went to the pregnancy center. It's the same kind of concept that Christ didn't leave her where she was, her life was transformed, and she got reconnected physically, emotionally, spiritually, and socially.

When she went back to the town, after that transformation, she wasn't an outcast anymore. She wasn't coming back to the well during the hottest part of the day, all alone, at-risk and vulnerable. Why? Because she got reconnected into the community. We know that because when Christ came to her town, hundreds and hundreds of people were saved, and if they truly were saved, then who helped connect them to Christ? It was her! So, you got to believe that the next time that she went to the well, she wasn't by herself, that she was reconnected into the community of women. She was reconnected to the community and to society. She was transformed.

That's the piece that's really important. It's really the extension where the pregnancy center then entrusts the woman to the Church and the people within the Church.

When the people in the church start to think about this more from a discipleship standpoint, they realize that we need to walk alongside this person. This is what it means to be in a discipleship relationship; you're going to be helping that person with their physical, emotional, spiritual, and social needs. And that is not a temporary relationship; it's an ongoing relationship where you're trying to get that person to move from the pregnancy to the Church to meet those other needs; pregnancy centers can't do all that. They're not designed to do that. The pregnancy center is primarily focused on mother and baby from conception to birth; they are not designed to fulfill the Great Commission.

We're not just trying to make sure that a child has life. We want to make sure that a child has abundant life, consistent with God's design. This is why we have to connect those we serve, both men and women, to the Church.

When Jesus engaged people, what did He do? The first thing He did was have compassion for them. He met them at their point of need. And that offered them hope.

I loved Roland's message; it confirmed to me and Lighthouse that we were headed in the right direction.

## The Gospel With Grace

Oftentimes in pregnancy centers, women come to Christ. Through their twice-a-month visits, they develop a relationship with their peer counselor where they hear the gospel and a decision is made for Christ. That's fantastic, but we can't stop there. Now that young woman needs discipleship; if she's not discipled, then she may be saved, but her life may not be transformed.

Christ's commission to the Church was to go and make disciples, not to *only* go and lead people to salvation or go save babies. That means that our commission is to make disciples of the mother and her child so they can have an abundant life in Christ, *and* help them overcome the trauma of abuse and the vicious cycle of generational poverty.

In this way, we apply the fullness of the gospel to our pregnancy center ministry and the Church.

## Easier Said Than Done

Biblical principles are easy to teach but sometimes difficult to apply to our daily lives. For example, we may teach a woman that sex outside of marriage is a sin, that God designed sex for marriage. It's a simple concept to understand, but it's not easy to live out when marriage and families are nonexistent in your community. We also know that families in poverty without a male in the household are at greater risk for violence, so we must remember that the man in her house meets her need for protection. How can she apply that principle to her life without support and role models to help her do that?

As we approach this ministry with the gospel, we also have to approach it with much grace, understanding that she's not living our lives in our environment with our safety and resources; she's living a completely different life than we are. She may want to be obedient in that area of her life, but she may not feel safe acting on it at the time.

We need humility and grace to seek to understand what life looks like in the context and in the culture and communities that we are serving so that we can approach it with awareness, understanding, and grace. This allows us to see that perhaps some of the choices that are being made are out of a necessity that we don't have to grapple with on a day-to-day basis.

Some of the choices for survival look very different and could actually be challenging to our moral values, but within the construct that these women are living, they're absolutely within their realm of reality and possibility, simply because that's what life requires for them to survive and we are always going to choose survival.

When we have a clear understanding of the environment that the women we serve are living in, we don't say or think things like, "Now that you know better, do better." The journey from hurt and bad habits to hopefulness in Christ is a long and sometimes messy one. It requires our steadfast support to keep the women and men we serve stumbling in the right direction.

Dr. Ruby Payne's book, *"A Framework For Understanding Poverty"* tells us that poverty is a culture and helps us understand how culture is a part of the very fabric of our lives. To remove yourself from culture, to remove yourself from a way of being that has been ingrained into who you are, is a very difficult thing.

There are going to be aspects and elements that remain as remnants. However we will focus on what we know is the right path and point people in that direction.

We have to recognize the need for a huge space for grace. It is not to condone a behavior that is a poor choice but to acknowledge that we are all powerless without the help of Jesus Christ, as well as each individual who invests in our lives. These women need someone they can reach out to when they are wobbly in their walk, who will help shore them up when they want to go back to the habit or the behavior that kept them from living their most abundant life. Our support must be a commitment to come along for the long and messy haul.

One of our workshop participants corrected me once when I said that knowledge was power. She said, "No, knowledge is not power; applied knowledge is power." That was a huge eye-opener for me because I realized that just because we taught them something or we modeled a behavior, didn't mean they were enabled to apply it in their lives.

You could know something, but not be in the environment in which you can apply it; you just can't apply knowledge across the board. There are obstacles and sometimes even danger to applying that knowledge in certain environments. We have to demonstrate patience and grace when we see that a woman knows things and has even seen you model them, but does not have the ability to apply them.

When we look at the Scriptures, and we see how Jesus walked with the chosen twelve, we realize there were many times that Jesus had to say, "let me remind you of what I taught you. How many times do I have to teach you this? Remember, when I showed you how to do this?"

Even with Jesus modeling and living with them, He had to constantly remind them. He specifically invited those He called to be on the journey with Him to leave their environments and come away and walk a journey with Him. They were invited to eat and sleep and be on the same path. Even with that level of intimacy, those who were walking and being discipled by Jesus Christ were prone to go back to their past behavior. They would forget what they had been taught, or not be able to apply what they had just seen, whether it was rebuking the devil, or being mindful that Jesus welcomed the sick and needy.

## Mentoring Makes The Difference

At RENEW Life Center, we use the term mentoring because if you ask a young woman who is struggling to survive if she wants to be discipled, the answer will most likely be no, she has other things on her mind. But if you offer her mentoring to help her reach her goals, the response is most frequently yes. Our prayer is that mentorship turns into discipleship, and more often than not, it does.

Much of what we do feels like we're parenting parents. Individuals who have chosen parenthood don't necessarily have the upbringing to be a responsible parent. The same way we parent our children by lovingly teaching, repeating, and reminding, we are in a way, with respect for their age, parenting the parents we serve. This is not inviting you into a relationship with a hierarchy; it is coming alongside another individual. It's an apprenticeship, it's a mentorship, it's discipleship. You respect them for the individual that they are, and acknowledge that they are separate and different from you. You are not personally responsible for them, but you have a responsibility to them because you have a responsibility to our Savior Jesus Christ.

*We invite you as a pro-life advocate into a life-changing ministry opportunity.*

Mentoring has been around for centuries; it's attributed to when King Odysseus left his young son in the care of his friend, Mentor. A mentor is someone who helps another learn the ways of the world or specific tasks. In a similar way, discipleship helps another learn the ways of Christ. At RENEW, a woman may have a primary and secondary mentor and at times, a tutor as well. She will gain a group of people to surround her and support her in her journey.

It's not a mentor's job to solve the mom's problems. The mentor helps the woman find solutions and guides her in developing problem-solving skills. However, a mentor will help her create SMART (**S**pecific, **M**easurable, **A**chievable, **R**elevant, and **T**ime-bound) goals and provide guidance, support, and encouragement as she sets out to meet milestones that lead to a healthy and stable home for her child, and ultimately a relationship with Jesus Christ.

We invite you as a pro-life advocate into a journey alongside a woman or man who has chosen life; we invite you into a life-changing missionary opportunity.

You might think of missionaries as people who serve outside of our country, but you could be a missionary to the urban city that is just a couple of miles away from your home. It's a full-time job for some people, and it's a volunteer opportunity for others. Either way, we need "manpower" to be able to provide the long-term care that we want to commit to for these young families. If we open our eyes and hearts to the pain, suffering, and abuse endured by the women and children we serve, if we allow God to use us as part of His plan to redeem and restore, we would see a greater number of lives transformed and connected to the community that is the Church, we would see whole cities transformed.

I was in my office one day when a local school nurse called and said the mother of a couple of boys in her school was in her office and that this woman needed a lot of help. One of the other moms in the school told her that the pregnancy resource center she was visiting referred her to *RENEW Life* and that our classes and mentoring changed her life.

Although the people we target to serve are women and men referred to us by the pregnancy resource center, we also get calls from other sources looking for support services for women. The nurse asked about our *Getting Ahead* program and wanted to know if we were still accepting applications. I told her a class was starting soon, so this woman had to come in that day to fill out an application and get interviewed for consideration into the program.

About an hour later, a petite and very thin woman walked in. She looked like a frightened little girl. I sat across from Julie during the interview. I could see her hands were trembling, and I sensed God tell me to "hug her." That was a strange thought for me; I'm not a hugger, especially when it comes to strangers. Besides, this was a professional interview. I wasn't going to hug her.

"Hug her!" I felt God say again and again, and repeatedly I thought "no." This internal dialogue went on throughout the entire interview. She shared that she was on the verge of being evicted for the seventeenth time in five years. She has no family in this country, and the boys' father abandoned them a long time ago. It was clear to me; this woman did not need a class. She needed a miracle, an advocate to intervene and try to secure viable housing for her and her children.

As the interview wrapped up, I told her that she could join our class and that I would accompany her to court for her eviction hearing to see if there was anything that could be done. As I reached out to shake her hand, the words "hug her" were still swirling around my heart.

As she was about to walk out the door, I said to her, "Hey, can I give you a hug?"

She darted back and hugged me like she was clinging onto a life preserver. At that moment, I felt the bottomless pit of need she had, and it wasn't just the immediate need for a secure home; she needed so much more. She sobbed as she held me. I had to fight back the tears. She thanked me for the hug and said she really needed it; she said she couldn't remember the last time she was hugged.

## She's Not Alone

The court date came around, and I accompanied her to court. She thanked me profusely for going with her. I told her that I didn't know if there was anything I could do to help, and she said, "That's OK, I'm just glad that I'm not here alone."

That's all she wanted, not to be alone. It's her turn before the judge, and they want her to pay $3,200 before 5 p.m., or she has to vacate the apartment. I asked for more time to try to come up with the money, but no, 5 p.m. was the deadline. I run a small nonprofit, and I didn't have an extra $3,200, so I took her to

Catholic Charities, thinking that they may help her immediately, but it would take a couple of weeks for them to get a check to her.

Next, I took her to the Department of Children and Families. I explained her situation and asked if they could help her; the response was no. I asked if they could place her and the boys in a shelter. The caseworker responded that they were out of shelter and motel vouchers, and then she added, "If she can't find a place to stay, we'll have to take possession of the boys." I was shocked at the callousness of this caseworker.

It's easy to assume that social services are in abundance, that shelters are free and safe, and that anyone can just walk into one at any time. This couldn't be further from the truth. While I stood there feeling helpless as she wept, she tells me she's grateful she's not alone.

Three days later, I pulled up to her house, and there she stood on the sidewalk with her two boys and all of her possessions out on the curb. I asked her what was going to happen to all of her things, and she said, "Once I leave, the neighbors will pick through my stuff and take what they want."

This was surreal to me. I have never seen or experienced anything like this, but now I know that it goes on every day in cities across our country. I couldn't bear the thought of her losing everything again, so I suggested that she select what was most important to her and put it in my minivan. We couldn't save everything, but we could save some of her treasured items. Once the items were loaded in the van, I drove them to a motel for the night. I bought them a pizza and some soda, and I told her I'd see her the next day to continue to try to figure out what to do. As I drove home, I felt sick. Is this the best I could do for them? Is this the best the body of Christ can offer the widow and the orphan? It was a long restless night for me, yet I'm sure it was far worse for them.

Julie and her kids spent several days in the motel while we tried to find a solution. RENEW was paying $120 a night for the motel, and we couldn't keep doing that for much longer. We got excited when a donor offered to cover the security deposit and first month's rent for an apartment for her, but questioned how she would keep up with the rent? She hadn't finished high school, she did not have any marketable job skills, the only job she ever had was cleaning, and she couldn't afford an apartment on just that. On top of that with her long list of evictions, no one reputable would be willing to rent to her without a huge upfront payment.

The money I had to pay for the motel was drying up quickly, and I lay awake in bed wondering what would happen to them if we couldn't find a long-term solution, fast. I had a thought; just down the hall in my house were two empty bedrooms, they had been empty for years. But it's crazy to bring people you don't really know into your home, isn't it? If you come from a background of poverty like my husband and I do, it's not so crazy.

We both remember times in our childhood when someone we didn't know was sleeping on the couch or even on the floor. There's an unspoken rule among the poor; you always share what you have because you never know when you'll be the one with the need. My husband had been hearing me talk about Julie and her boys for several days, and he knew how my heart was broken for them. So when I asked him if I could bring them home with me just for a few nights while we figured things out, he didn't hesitate to say yes.

I could still cry when I remember Julie's face as she sat on the bedroom floor at my house. She didn't want to sit on the bed; she was a broken mess of a woman. She felt ashamed to be taken in by strangers, she felt guilty for what she had put her children through, and she felt rejected and abandoned by the man she thought loved her. I didn't know what to say to her, so I sat next to her and said nothing; she looked at me and thanked me for not leaving her alone.

Three years have passed since that night, and Julie and her boys are still living with us. I can't begin to tell you how they have blessed our lives. God has taught me, my husband, and our nineteen-year-old son so much through this experience. He used it to mold us and teach us how to love how He loves. It wasn't always easy; early on, there were times when I was so frustrated with her. I would think, "Why isn't she getting things done quicker? Why can't she make up her mind? Why is she still crying over that man? We've opened our home to her, she doesn't have to worry about being in the street, we're providing everything for them, why doesn't she take advantage of this opportunity and get her GED?"

The questions went on and on, and my frustration grew and grew to the point that I wanted to throw my hands up in the air and give up on her. But every time I wanted to give up and tell her this is not working out, I could sense God asking me what would happen if I gave up on you? I came to terms that it was not my project to fix her. I just had to love her like God does, unconditionally. So began my journey to learn to love Julie unconditionally regardless of whether she met my expectations or not, but simply because she was His daughter and He entrusted her to me that day He said: "hug her."

Through this experience, I'm happy to tell you that I've learned that the best way to help transform someone's life is to love them like God does. I figured if they left my house with nothing else, I want them to leave knowing Jesus. They go to church with us every Sunday. The boys attended the youth group and quickly made friends. I sent them to Christian camp during summer vacations, and one of them received Jesus as Savior!

Julie has expressed a desire to be baptized, she got hired in a local daycare center, she's passed two out of the five courses for her GED, and she's a beautiful vibrant woman who I now call my daughter. Her boys say that they're living their dream life, and she says I'm the mother she never had, and I have an even bigger bonus family. God and Julie have taught me so much through this experience that I don't think I could have learned any other way. It has been messy, frustrating, and glorious. God is so good.

I'm not advocating that everyone should take women and children into their homes. This is just my story. But ask yourself, how can you be a part of someone's transformation journey? How can God use you to bring love and hope where there is none?

## Jesus With Skin On

In a candid conversation with Veronica, one of our longtime mentors, we talked about the vital role mentors play in the development and transformation of the women we serve. I found what she said to be profound. Her insights strengthened the conviction I have about the important role the Church plays in our ministry.

**Veronica:**
When the women we serve cry out for help, that cry is not, "Where are you, God?"

"Rather, it is: "Who are you today?" They are essentially asking what form is help embodying today? Are you a pastor today in my crisis? Are you my mentor today in my situation? When a woman is going through a difficult time, asking her to hold on to the feeling or knowledge that God is with her is not enough. She needs more than a feeling; she needs physical evidence. She needs to take hold of someone and feel their presence, an actual body. It has to be someone who she can see with her eyes, who she can truly be in the moment with, talk with, and relate to so that she can say: "God put this person in my life at that moment to impact me, and get me through that season."

"Then when she looks back, she can say, "When I was going through something, God put a mentor, God put a sister in Christ in my life." In reality, it's not just a person He put, but a true servant of God who could be filled up by Him to be used in her life at that moment. God does this because she needs that more than a feeling. For God to be real, she needs evidence of God, such as a servant of God appearing in the flesh. We can tell her to pray and read her Bible, but sometimes a still, small voice isn't enough; sometimes it has to be a person. The best example of that is Jesus Christ Himself.

"God talked for thousands of years, and the time came where he had to come in the form of a human being to embody the son of man and be the son of God so that we can relate to Him. The knowledge and feeling of God weren't enough; religious leaders weren't enough, that's why today we have Jesus Christ. We also have ambassadors of Christ around us all the time; they are called believers.

"In 1 Corinthians 14:33 scripture says that God is a God of order, and He wants to be able to pour into the lives of these women so that their lives can have order and they can continually walk in the way that He has for them. The only way they can replicate this in their own lives is to have a living example. Where is that example constantly being played out? In the church! How are they going to know the God of order and peace if they're not connected with His Church?"

Being connected is not a one-way street, however. Getting someone to come to service on Sunday will not create a connection or transform their life. They may find moments of faith and hope in those services, but the only way for real transformation to occur is to be in a relationship with those in the Church; brothers and sisters in Christ who are committed to showing their faith through their actions, not just their words. What is your threshold for offering support and guidance to single moms or co-parenting couples in your church who are just keeping their heads above water? This type of discipleship is the core of how poverty can be alleviated, not by money or policy, but by the body of Christ investing time and energy in those who struggle spiritually and economically.

Representing Jesus well and approaching ministry through the lens of the gospel is far easier in theory than in practice. In over twenty years of ministry, I have found that when humanity is on full display, it can be messy and hard to endure. Those are the moments we have to embrace Galatians 6:9, Let us not grow weary in doing good, for in due time we will reap a harvest if we do not give up.

# Chapter 5

# Bridging the Gap Between Short-Term Support and Long-Term Sustainability

> *"Our success in influencing others is in proportion to their belief in our belief in them."*
>
> **Henry Drummond**

How did we get here? How did this happen? Those were my thoughts after reading Armenia's email. We did a great job of leading her to choose life, but then we dropped the ball. My particular pregnancy center at the time didn't have many resources to offer her, and maybe other pregnancy centers would have had the ability to give her the items she listed in the email without much difficulty, but the real need was greater than that.

She needed much more than just material items to care for her baby. She needed to be reassured over and over that she made the right choice, and nobody was doing that for her. There was no

> *To thrive, families need a strong safety net and support system.*

soothing voice, no reassuring person walking with her through the wilderness she found herself in.

In a recent conversation with Armenia, I mentioned to her that at the time I received her email, I had been in the ministry for eight years, and in those years, we had served at least 7,000 women. "Why did it take 7,000 women for me to get one email like yours?" She responded:

"I almost didn't send that email. I sent it because I thought that hearing no, we can't help you would be easier for me. Or if I did not receive a response from you, it would be an obvious NO. I would then know that I'm not going to waste my time and ever go back there again. Plus, my pregnancy was high risk at the time, and I was bedridden.

I needed help, I couldn't get up and emailing you was my only way to reach people who I thought could help me. I knew about Planned Parenthood, but I wasn't sure if they had anything to offer me besides an abortion. At that moment, I was not sure about continuing with the pregnancy, and I know they were good at persuading you to abort. I was still at the stage where it was possible to do it; I was afraid they would talk me into it."

I asked her what would've happened if I hadn't responded. She said:

"I was looking into possibly placing the baby for adoption. But the only thing is, I don't know if I could've lived with myself."

I was curious, so I asked her why some women believe that having an abortion is easier than making an adoption plan.

She responded, "Because you will always know that your child is out there, and you will ache to be with your child. You will have a hole in your heart for the rest of your life. Because of that, we think it's easier to abort and shut our conscience. It's the same reason why some women don't want to sell their eggs, although they can get five to ten thousand dollars for them; a piece of them would be out there. They could make money off of it, but they still don't do it."

I told her I was glad I responded.

"Yes, me too," she said. "I slept with the laptop open, hoping you would respond."

## RENEW Life Center Is Founded

My volunteers and I gathered together, we prayed, and we asked God to show us the needs single women and couples faced when confronted with an unplanned pregnancy. We asked Him to show us how we should address those needs. He answered. One day He impressed these verses from the book of Isaiah upon my heart:

> The Spirit of the Sovereign Lord is on me,
>      because the Lord has anointed me
>      to proclaim good news to the poor.
> He has sent me to bind up the brokenhearted,
>      to proclaim freedom for the captives
> and release from darkness for the prisoners, [a]
>      ² to proclaim the year of the Lord's favor
>      and the day of vengeance of our God,

to comfort all who mourn,
³and provide for those who grieve in Zion—
to bestow on them a crown of beauty
instead of ashes,
the oil of joy
instead of mourning,
and a garment of praise
instead of a spirit of despair.
They will be called oaks of righteousness,
a planting of the Lord
for the display of his splendor.

**Isaiah 61: 1-3 (NIV)**


In those few verses God answered our prayer. Here is how we personalized those verses:

The Spirit of the Sovereign Lord is leading and equipping us, because the Lord has called us to share the gospel to single moms and couples who have chosen life.

He has sent us to help put back together the broken hearts of women that feel betrayed and abandoned, by pointing them to Jesus.

We are to proclaim freedom from condemnation and the oppression of poverty; to bring light and hope for those suffering from loneliness, and depression.

To teach them to trust in God's grace and mercy, and to rest in the assurance of his promises.

To comfort all who mourn the loss of relationships
or the future they fear is lost because of the
unplanned pregnancy.

We are to place on them a crown of beauty, instead of
shame, the oil of joy instead of mourning, and a garment of praise instead of a spirit of despair.

They will be restored, and called strong and mag-
nificent, known for their integrity, justice, and right
standing with God; a work of the Lord

That He may be glorified

The first three verses of Isaiah 61 became our marching orders. We founded RENEW Life Center to be a vehicle through which the Church can reach women like Armenia and fill the gap that exists between the choice for life and the lifetime ahead. In collabora- tion with the Church, we hope to assure these single women and couples that they have a continuous stream of support. A constant stream of access to resources such as physical, emotional, social, and most important spiritual resources. These needs are not filled within their families or their communities; without the support of the body of Christ, many of these needs will go unmet.

## Our Agendas vs. God's Will

In her email, Armenia states that her mother became too busy for her. We can all relate to being busy; I'm sure as you're reading this, you are also thinking of a few other things you should be doing instead. I know that my natural tendency is to want to get things done; checking items off on my to-do list gives me great satisfaction. And when I'm in the "groove" of getting things done, I hate to be interrupted; I once complained about that to Joan, the pregnancy center director, where I volunteered.

I still remember her words, "Did you know that most of Jesus' ministry was an interruption?" I asked her what she meant by that, and she responds, "Jesus was usually on His way somewhere, or teaching and even praying when He's interrupted with a request to meet a need."

Wow, I never noticed that before. From then on, when I read my Bible, I looked for the interruptions that were occurring in Jesus' life on earth. I learned that He valued caring for the lost and hurting more than getting to His destination on time or any other item on His agenda. If we loosen our grip on our to-do list just a bit and allow God to interrupt our busy lives, we can significantly impact women like Armenia and even entire families. 1 John 2:17 (NLT) reminds us that "…this world is fading away, along with everything that people crave. But anyone who does what pleases God will live forever."

At RENEW Life, we created an environment where single moms and families can feel supported by believers who provide guidance for the journey that lies ahead. Families come to RENEW looking for help in becoming self-sustaining; it's dehumanizing to be dependent on the government; nobody wants to be on welfare for a lifetime. Some are believers, and others are not.

Still, as we help them achieve the self-sustainability they want most, it opens the doors to the gospel message for those who don't know the Lord, and it brings opportunity for discipleship for those who do. When we view discipleship as something that grows their relationship with the Lord *and* helps them take

steps towards creating stable homes and achieving self-sustainability, we demonstrate that we care for every aspect of their life.

## Poverty And Shame

I remember as a little girl, my mom would have me miss school
so I could accompany her to her welfare appointments. Back in
those days, a Spanish speaking social worker was a rarity, and
they did not have translators. I remember the dirty plastic chairs,
the grueling questions, the condescending looks, and the obvious
shame my mother felt. I had to translate things for her that she
probably never wanted me to know. I remember the long silent
walks home. I shared her shame.

Today, in some ways, it's even worse. There are plenty of
bilingual social workers, but instead of just having to share your
most intimate details with one social worker, you have to share
them with three. You have one social worker for your cash assistance (TANF), one for your food stamps (SNAP), and yet another
for your housing assistance (TRA). Every time she sees a different social worker, she relives her trauma and shame. At some
point in her life, she may think that self-sustainability is just not
an option; it's just not attainable for her. If a woman like Armenia, who now has a Master's degree and a full-time job, is still
struggling to be self-sustaining, can you imagine the chances of a
twenty or thirty-year-old woman without a high school diploma?

## Transformation Requires The Church

So how can the Church get involved in this daunting mission?
The first step is to learn about poverty. Even if you're reading

this and you're thinking, I grew up in poverty, I know all about it. I promise you; you don't. I truly did not understand my family dynamics and the effect poverty had on all of us, until I read Dr. Payne's book, *"A Framework for Understanding Poverty."* She also wrote a book specifically for churches titled *"What Every Church Member Should Know About Poverty."*

There are many other great books on the topic that would be very helpful to read, and some are listed in the appendix, but I want to caution you about two things: first, don't get stuck on learning and feel you have to read every book ever written on the subject. Second, don't just learn from books; learn by jumping right in and creating relationships of mutual respect with people in poverty; they have so much to teach us.

The women who visit Lighthouse Pregnancy Resource Center have the good fortune that they didn't just step into a beautiful, state-of-the-art facility, but they stepped into one that recognizes their long-term needs. There's a seamless transition between Lighthouse's pregnancy services and RENEW's long-term support through workshops, leadership development, mentoring and discipleship. Our collaboration has led us to see a spiritual and financial transformation in the lives of the women we serve. But in order for these transformations to happen, we are heavily dependent on the Church. It requires a small army of volunteers who genuinely want to build a relationship with these women, not take them on as a project or mission, but genuinely want to befriend them for a season and maybe even a lifetime.

Yes, I said a lifetime. Nowadays, that seems a little extreme. We live in a culture where we think microwaves are slow. We live with the idea that if we do our "job" well, we can get it done quickly and move on to the next person or the next mission. We have been conditioned by "day of service" events to develop a "tourist mindset" of our Christian life of service, seeing it as less of a pilgrimage and more of a DIY project. We want casual commitments and immediate results. We desire the outcomes derived from discipline but fail to invest the time, preferring instead to fast forward to the fruit without nurturing the root. I'll admit that I was unknowingly falling into that mindset even while I was working in ministry. I wanted quick results.

As you walk alongside these moms and families, you will learn more about yourself and God than you could ever imagine. It will be your long apprenticeship to grow in holiness. For me, it's in service to these families that I am able to see the Biblical principles I hear my pastor preach about on Sunday come to life on Monday, Tuesday, Wednesday, and every other day of the week. It's in serving that I am able to pour out what has been poured into me. Serving in ministry in both volunteer and staff roles has been the fertile ground God has used to grow and develop my faith, and I suspect it would be the same for you.

I mentioned earlier that RENEW Life Center was founded to fill the gap between the choice women and men make for life and the lifetime after that choice. What's needed to fill that gap is the body of Christ to use their unique gifts in helping us provide the educational workshops and services these families need to grow in Christ and grow in economic stability. There is a role for everyone.

Is your heart leaning towards serving women facing an unplanned pregnancy and parenting concerns? Then contact your local pregnancy center; there are many volunteer roles for you to choose from. Do you have a special interest in helping teen moms? Young*Lives* is a ministry of Young Life focused on reaching teen moms by entering their world, modeling the unconditional love of Christ, and encouraging them to become the women and mothers God created them to be.

If your local pregnancy center doesn't already have a Young-*Lives* club, how about you and your church start one? Maybe it's the thought of the hardships caused by poverty that grips your heart, and you want to help moms create economically stable homes for their babies to thrive. Well, contact RENEW and get plugged into one of our many volunteer roles. If your local pregnancy center doesn't offer expanded services like those provided by RENEW, then why not look into starting something similar?

## From Surviving to Thriving

RENEW equips single moms and couples who have chosen life to overcome generational poverty and build healthy relationships. Our educational programs, mentoring/discipleship, and leadership training transform lives and restore hope and dignity through the gospel and support in their journey to self-sustainability. As a result, these families experience a shift from a survival mindset to a thriving mindset. There is also a shift in how they view relationships and marriage – these shifts in thinking lead to reduced dependence on government assistance, and emotionally and economically stable homes.

According to the Guttmacher Institute, one of the top three reasons for having an abortion is the inability to afford a child. We often hear stories of young women born and raised in poverty who are aspiring for more. Then, when faced with an unexpected pregnancy while in college, their world falls apart, and their dreams for an outcome better than what they were born into are in great danger. We want to inspire these women to believe that achieving economic stability is possible while choosing life.

When poverty is generational, it's a chronic condition that keeps churning out more poverty until "something" positive happens that interrupts the cycle. RENEW is that "something" that is interrupting poverty for our families. Poverty is an overwhelming issue, the magnitude of it almost paralyzes us from taking action. But when it comes to poverty, I want to narrow your focus to the women and men who walk into your local pregnancy resource center and choose life. Let's not only lead them to choose life, let's lead them to a life more abundant.

So how do we do that? At RENEW, we have curated workshops and Bible studies that address the special needs of the women and families we serve:

**Money & Me**: A financial literacy workshop created specifically for low-income adults.

**Mom as Gatekeeper**: A workshop that helps break down barriers between mothers and fathers by addressing what is known as Maternal Gatekeeping. Maternal gatekeeping is common in poverty, where children have been raised solely by their mothers. Young women are raised to believe that a father isn't really necessary.

**Think Differently**: A Bible study that challenges the faulty thinking that has been running our lives.

**_Leadership Development_**: Various leadership development workshops to help our moms and dads reach their peak potential.

**_Getting AHEAD in a Just Gettin' By World:_**
Getting AHEAD is our main workshop, which we believe is foundational in getting people out of poverty. What's so special about Getting AHEAD (GA)? What makes GA different from other workshops is that the focus is not on poverty symptoms, such as unemployment, homelessness, and limited education. It addresses the root causes of poverty, which can be summed up as a knowledge gap, and provides practical steps and tools to overcome it.

Programs that address the symptoms of poverty are critically important; the problem is that they're building on an unstable foundation. We end up with people with an education, a job, and a home – still operating from a survival mindset. It's only a matter of time before everything falls apart, and they're back at square one.

Take Armenia, for example. She had a college education; actually, she had an advanced degree, she had a career, and to quote her, "she was doing what she was supposed to be doing." In other words, she was getting things done. Yet, she's facing many of the same challenges as those who don't. Why? Because poverty does not end with a college education or a job. It ends with a mindset shift. The *Getting AHEAD* workshop helps the participant make that mindset shift.

The *Getting AHEAD* workshop is intense, it's not for everyone. To participate, you need a referral from your Lighthouse peer counselor, or another RENEW partner agency. Then you have to complete an application, followed by an interview. Why do we do all of this? We do it because helping people overcome poverty is expensive, and we don't merely want to fill a seat; we want to bring about real results.

We are looking for women and men, who are ready to face the hard truth about their economic condition, individuals who are ready to dig deep and analyze how they contributed to their current situation, and also explore how community conditions and government policy also contribute to chronic poverty. And finally, we are looking for people who are ready, willing, and able to make BIG changes in their lives.

Once accepted into the program, the journey begins! For the next ten weeks, we read, research, and report on the causes of poverty. Understanding what causes poverty helps participants from generational poverty, understand how their family of origin functioned and how they got to where they are today.

Although raised in poverty, I never really understood it until I went through the training to teach the Getting AHEAD material. As I went through the training, my upbringing and my parents' choices began to make sense. I quickly realized that there is a huge knowledge gap in poverty that most people don't know exists, not even the poor themselves. The topics discussed in the workshop are basic life skills topics that any middle-income teenager would be well aware of, but it's eye-opening information for our participants.

One comment we frequently hear in class is, "Why don't they teach us this in school?" The answer is that they believe you already know it, that it's taught at home; for example, planning for your future. As a teenager growing up in poverty, I didn't know that my future was up to me. I didn't know that I could dream, make choices and make plans that would lead to a successful life;

planning for the future was not taught in my home. I'm sure that somewhere along my childhood, I must have had teachers tell me that I can do and be anything if I set my mind to it, but I didn't believe them; my home life didn't reflect that. That message was for other people, not girls like me.

In the Getting AHEAD workshop, participants learn that to get out of poverty, they have to build on eleven key areas of their lives. It goes far beyond gaining employment; we address the support and resources needed to keep the job, advance their skills, and create relationships that will foster their social and mental growth.

They also learn that different environments operate from a different set of rules of engagement. In the academic and professional world, the rules of engagement are based on achievement. How does someone from generational poverty successfully navigate that environment when the only rules of engagement they know are survival based? These topics and the many others that follow help properly equip the families we serve to enter unfamiliar territory and navigate it with confidence.

After completing our Getting Ahead workshop, graduates have the opportunity to be paired with tutors or mentors who will serve as friends, guides, and role models on their journey to faith and self-sustainability.

## Getting By Before Getting Ahead

Getting out of poverty is hard work, and it's scary, especially when your safety net of government assistance is quickly disappearing.

Once a mom enters the workforce and is fortunate enough to get a childcare subsidy, her other benefits such as SNAP and TANF begin to decline. Although social workers will tell you that it is a slow decline, those on the receiving end would not agree with that. Let's take Gina, for example. She was a mom to three small children when she first came to Lighthouse for a pregnancy test. She was born and raised in Paterson, and although she had her first baby as a teenager, she managed to graduate high school and get certified as a dental assistant.

Life was going pretty well for her, so she decided to pursue her lifelong dream of moving to North Carolina to give her children a better life. She moved with her three children and her boyfriend, and for a while, life was great. They had a lovely apartment with a playground for the kids, they both had jobs, and they were even able to buy a used car. But then her car broke down, and they didn't have the money to fix it, so she started taking the bus to work.

Unfortunately, she had to walk the kids to school and then grab the bus to work. The bus schedule did not align with the time she had to be at work, so she was often late. Her boss gave her a warning about her lateness, so she explained her situation and requested that her schedule be adjusted, but he did not budge. After several warnings from her boss, she was fired. With no car and no job, she could not make rent payments and eventually got evicted, even though her boyfriend was working and contributing to their expenses.

Then her boyfriend disappeared. Why? Maybe he only wanted to be with her while it was easy and didn't want to deal with the chaos. Perhaps he was helpless in rescuing his family, which made him feel so impotent and ashamed that he couldn't face them; we don't know.

All Gina could do was stuff her children's backpacks with all the clothes she could squeeze in and get on a train back to

Paterson, New Jersey. She had no choice but to move into her parents' house, a very toxic environment. Her family mocked her for daring to dream of a better life. "We knew you would be back with your tail between your legs," they told her arrogantly.

Shortly afterward, she started to suspect that she was pregnant, and that was how she ended up at Lighthouse sitting across from me. By this time, I had served in pregnancy center ministries for 15 years, so when I tell you that this was one of the hardest intakes I have ever done, I don't say that lightly. It was as if she was drowning, and I was a life raft that she could cling to long enough to share her story before she lost her grip. But instead of going under, she gets pulled up onto the raft and hears, "It's going to be ok; we've got you."

Gina's pregnancy test was positive; the test result left her feeling fear and despair. How could she have another baby now? I told her about Lighthouse's programs that would provide emotional and material support throughout her pregnancy and the baby's first year. Then I told her about RENEW's programs and services that would support her in getting back on her feet to come back even stronger and more stable than she was before.

She asked me how long RENEW would provide emotional support and guidance. I told her for as long as it takes for her and her children to feel safe and secure. And even after that, I would hope to have the privilege of watching her and her children flourish. Through the tears, I saw a little comfort and a spark of hope.

Gina wanted to sign up for our Getting Ahead class right away. I told her she should wait until after the baby was born because her due date was during the course's tail end, and she would miss out on the final sessions. It was our fall session, and classes were on Mondays and Thursdays, but she insisted and made her case: "I'm due right around Thanksgiving; if I give birth between the Monday before Thanksgiving and that Friday, I can be in class on Monday. I would only miss two sessions, and I can make up the missed assignments." Was she kidding me? Nope, she was dead serious. Although I thought that was impossible, I loved her excitement and enthusiasm. I didn't have the heart to say no, so against my better judgment; I enrolled her in the class.

Gina started the class, had incredible breakthroughs, made new friends, received tons of love and encouragement, and gave birth the Wednesday before Thanksgiving! And just as she promised, she showed up to class on Monday morning! By the time Gina graduated from the workshop, the girl was on fire! She had three job interviews the week after graduating and acquired a full-time job the week after that. Great story, right?

## But Wait, There's More...

Now, she would face obstacles that, if RENEW were not there to help her, she could never overcome on her own.

The first obstacle was childcare. Childcare costs are as much as $225 per child per week, although childcare subsidies are available for low-income families, some states have a waiting period of several months. If she is fortunate enough to apply without being placed on a waiting list, she still must provide two weeks' worth of pay stubs to get approved. So how does she pay for childcare during those two weeks? Thankfully because of the donations we received for our Bridge the Gap Fund, RENEW covered the cost of childcare for those two weeks. Had we not, Gina could not have accepted the job. Do you see the Catch-22 this creates?

The second obstacle is the reduction of her SNAP benefits. Gina was doing such a great job at work that she got a raise; her hourly pay went up by two dollars, from $15 an hour to $17. That's cause for a celebration, so we celebrated! A month later, Gina shows up at my office looking frantic and tells me she has to quit her job. "What?" I say, surprised and confused. She tells me that she received a letter from her SNAP benefits that now that she's had a pay increase, they would reduce her benefits from $700 a month to $450.

She's panic-stricken; her safety net of public assistance was rapidly disappearing. "I can barely make it as it is. How am I going to do it with less?" she cried. Here's the logic behind her wanting to leave her job: Gina knows that if she leaves her job, she will retain her $700 per month food benefit and Gina would also get TRA (temporary rental assistance), and she may even get some cash from TANF, but even if she didn't get the TANF, she has guaranteed food and housing for her children. She's not crazy; she's actually "poverty smart."

Our current regulations and policies around these assistance programs discourage people from working; it's safer and even saner to depend on the government for survival than to go out there and try to make it on your own.

I was trying to calm her down, but nothing I said mattered. She kept saying, "I have to quit! I have to quit!" Not knowing what else to say, I finally blurted out, "No! You're not going to quit, and I promise you, you and your kids will have plenty to eat".

As soon as the words left my mouth, I thought to myself, what did I just say? How am I going to keep that promise? But it worked. She calmed down and went back to work; she trusted me. Now I had to figure out how I was going to keep that promise.

Keeping in mind that we founded RENEW to be a conduit through which the Church can serve moms like Gina. I reached out to the Women's Ministry team leader from a church that regularly supported our ministry and told her Gina's story and the promise I had made. She immediately sprang into action, shared the need with the women's group, and developed a plan to provide weekly groceries to replace what Gina had lost by continuing to work. At the same time, Gina is connected with a mentor who takes her and her children to church. This is the Gospel in action; this is what a comprehensive approach to pro-life ministry looks like, and as Roland Warren would say, this is what it means to be pro- abundant life.

## The Bridge Out Of Poverty

Gina is still struggling to provide food for her children, pay the rent, and maintain a self-sufficient lifestyle as a single mother. Like all the women we serve she's stumbling in the right direction. Getting out of poverty is hard, breaking bad habits is even harder, and replacing an old mindset with a new way of thinking and living takes steadfast effort – and time. It takes much more time than we would like, but we commit to serve women like Gina with the same patience and grace God shows us all.

No matter how long the journey takes, every new skill, every new mindset change is passed to a mother's children. Her children learn the concepts, skills, and tools she's learning in her twenties or thirties at a much earlier age. Kerri, one of our first Getting Ahead graduates, said, "Since graduating, I have accomplished so much! One of the things I am most proud of is that after being unemployed for eight years, I finally have a job I love! I went from not having any confidence and feeling like my life was out of control to now walking with my head held high. Even more exciting is that I can pass on all I have learned to my children so they will have a leg up starting off their lives." That's not just one life transformed; that's lives changed for generations to come.

For the women and families, we serve at RENEW, knowing that they have people in their lives who care about their spiritual growth, their goals, and dreams while also connecting them to the resources to accomplish those goals means the world to them. It gives them hope for the future they have always dreamed of attaining.

One thing is sure; poverty is very lonely. Many of our graduates met their best friend at our Getting Ahead workshop; they finally have a friend who wants the same things they do: a better life for themselves and their children. They found a friend who will not criticize them for wanting more out of life, a friend who will cheer them on. Coupled with their relationship with their mentor, the RENEW staff, and a church, these relationships create a community around them that provides role models, resources, love, acceptance, and safety.

# The Bridge Out of Poverty

*Image adapted from SJC Bridges 2012

This diagram above shows you how quickly the safety net of necessary benefits (such as food stamps, rent subsidies, and childcare) are lost long before financial stability is achieved.

## Invisible Resources

Most people who are considered middle-income have resources that are almost invisible to them, meaning that they can sometimes take them for granted. But for someone in poverty, access to those resources can be the difference between surviving and thriving.

For example, you have a network of friends, colleagues, and other professionals who you can tap into when you have a need. Let's say you're looking for a job, so you contact a couple of old colleagues to see if they are hiring at their company. Or your friend owns a landscaping company, and you ask him if he can give your teenager a summer job. Those are resources that people in poverty often don't have.

Now imagine if you shared your network with someone in poverty; you ask your friend who owns the landscaping company if he would give your mentee an internship at his office to practice the office skills she's learned and have some experience she can put on a resume. It's connections like these that make the difference to an individual who wants to move from where they are to where they aspire to be.

It's the little things that often end up making the difference. When we donate clothes to the Salvation Army thrift store, we see it as gaining extra space in our closet, but for the mother who can buy those clothes at a low price and keep her kids warm all winter, it's nothing short of a miracle. When you donate a lawnmower to a church member trying to start his own lawn care service company, you are nurturing his right to dream and his desire to begin paying for his own needs.

# Chapter 6

# A Christian Approach to Choosing Life, Navigating Parenthood and Overcoming Poverty

*"Christian life isn't a one-person race. It's a relay. You are not alone; you're part of a team assembled by our unstoppable God to achieve his eternal purposes."*

**Christine Caine**

One of the most common verses used in the pro-life movement is Deuteronomy 30:19; you may be familiar with it. It says, *"This day I call the heavens and the earth as witnesses against you that I have set before you life and death, blessings and curses. Now choose life, so that you and your children may live".*

It wasn't until recently that I realized that there wasn't a period at the end of verse 19, and that verse 20 starts with "and" and it continues with *"that you may love the Lord your God, listen to his voice, and hold fast to him."*

> *Throughout the ages, the church has been involved in building culture, structuring society, and shaping the family.*

Wow, it says it right there; there is more to choosing life than living! There's an "and," and that's what this book is all about. It is also the "why" behind the work of RENEW and the reason we are so passionate and unapologetic about challenging Christians to see the bigger picture and participate more fully in the pro-abundant life mission.

I agree with Roland Warren, president of CareNet, when he says we should be "solving for heartbeats that are heaven-bound." Making life choices possible is crucial, but if our services and support stop there, it will likely be a messy, hard life that is not well lived. I get excited when I read Deuteronomy 30:19, and I let myself slide right into verse 20; that's where abundant life begins. It begins with loving God, listening to His voice, and holding fast to Him.

## The Pregnancy Center's Role

I interviewed Debbie Provencher, Executive Director of Lighthouse Pregnancy Resource Center in New Jersey. I asked her to tell us about the role pregnancy resource centers play in the comprehensive approach to pro-life ministry. She said:

> The pregnancy center comes alongside someone making a pregnancy decision. Our role is to help this person or couple assess their physical, emotional, and spiritual needs and strengths as they're making this important choice. We want to equip them with the resources to be able to choose life and to thrive as parents.

We're looking at their entire situation, and we're helping them slow down to do this, too. As I think about this, when people debate the abortion issue, when they talk about abortion and its rightness or wrongness, they're often approaching it from a theoretical standpoint. We're actually helping the real women and men who are making these decisions in the midst of complex situations. They're making these decisions with pressures from the outside, with the experiences in their life that have shaped them, their family of origin, their current circumstances, and especially the people in their lives right now who are either supportive or not in favor of this pregnancy. That's everything that comes to bear on their decision.

We're trying to help them look past the immediate fear, past the immediate circumstances and pressures to get a bigger, better perspective. Sometimes the woman or couple need help to realize that they already have the resources within them, but fear is clouding their judgment. It just takes someone to slow them down and say, 'Wow, the fact that you came here today looking for help means that you're already thinking like a mom. You started taking prenatal vitamins already because you care about your child's well-being.'

We are really helping parents get to the heart of who they are, to be able to sort through the complicated emotions that they're feeling. We don't want to see them make a quick decision they will regret, or a decision they can't commit to once they walk out our doors.

I think most pregnancy centers do a good job caring for the whole person. We recognize, like Jesus did when He stopped His preaching to feed the 5,000, that people can't hear us if they are hungry. They're not going to hear anything we're saying about life or about the gospel, until we take care of their most immediate needs. Jesus cared for people's whole needs, not just their spiritual needs. He took care of their physical needs, too."

I agreed with her point but felt there was a deeper complexity here, so I asked: "Pregnancy centers do a great job at meeting many of those immediate physical needs, but your role or mission is not to dive deep into them, correct? What I'm hoping people will understand is that in some areas, there's a gap. There's a misconception that after a woman walks into a pregnancy resource center everything's going to be okay.

Debbie responded:

There are needs our parents have that are greater than any one nonprofit can meet, or are outside the scope of our mission. At a staff meeting last week, at least four of the prayer requests were for women who are feeling pressured by their housing situations or financial hardships. One pregnant woman was happy just to be sleeping on a friend's couch, but that friend is getting evicted from her apartment.

Most of the challenges our moms face are related to housing and economic needs. Many of them are in unhealthy or abusive relationships, but they're tied to that person because of a housing need, or they're tied to their parents because of housing needs. The biggest

need I see over and over again, is the need for affordable, adequate housing for a mom and her child.

I remember 10 years ago; I spoke with the director of a
nonprofit ministry that offers housing and education
assistance to first-time moms. It was a wakeup call for
me because I was neglecting that piece of the overall
picture. Many pregnancy decisions are connected to
the woman's housing situation or to the person providing housing to the woman. So, it's all related to eco-
nomics. If a person can't get a job that adequately pays
the rent, then what?"

I asked Debbie what other needs clients at her center faced
that a pregnancy center isn't designed to meet.

She responded,

Jobs. If a mom wasn't already working, she will have
to look for a job, and if she's very pregnant and if she
already has another child to care for, you're thinking,
'This just isn't going to add up.' It's mainly financial
needs that are a pressing concern. We offer material
aid related to the pregnancy and to caring for a newborn. On occasion, we provide some emergency financial assistance for rent or utilities. But that assistance
is a bit like giving someone a fish today, without equipping them to fish for tomorrow and the day after that;
you're just making them more dependent on you or
someone else. This is why we chose to collaborate with
RENEW Life Center.

When you and the other founders of RENEW saw the problem of these unmet needs, you thought there must be a solution out there. So you searched, and you searched, and you found the Framework for Understanding Poverty curriculum. You identified the problem, but you didn't say, 'I have to be the only solution'; instead, you helped find the solution and brought it to the parents we serve. It's what I admired, and why I caught the vision.

As a pregnancy center, we want to excel. We want to improve those things that are within our wheelhouse, so to speak. But if there's a program or a ministry out there that's doing it better, and we can collaborate, then we will be better partnering together. This way, we don't have to create and oversee a whole new program ourselves; we can partner with others who are already doing it.

Since the founders of RENEW had already been in pregnancy center work, you identified a solution to a problem that we had all seen: the overwhelming financial situation so many of the parents we serve face. That's the reason they're coming to the center; it's because they lack the resources for their current or future children. Collaborating just makes so much sense. We don't have to be an expert in everything."

## The Benefits Of Collaboration And Christian Values

Indeed, we don't have to be experts in everything. God has equipped us with unique gifts and talents. We just have to put them to use.

When RENEW first began our collaboration with Lighthouse, we quickly realized that our program did not work well with the teen moms, but it worked great for a young woman in her twenties or older. We were excited when Lighthouse added the YoungLives program to their collaborative efforts so that teen moms could be reached. As the saying goes, teamwork makes the dream work.

But make no mistake, it won't be easy, especially if these women, whether teens or young adults, grew up in generational poverty. It's hard sometimes to get someone to focus on spiritual things, which are abstract, while she's drowning in concrete problems. So, at RENEW, we listen, we find out what issues are most pressing for her, what are her hopes and dreams, and then we help her address those issues.

We develop a relationship with her through our workshops and mentoring that are designed to help her overcome poverty. Some will achieve that, and others won't, but we pray that all will develop a lifelong relationship with God. Whether she overcomes poverty or not, having a relationship with Jesus Christ will not only transform her spiritually but will also transform her experience in poverty.

As I reflected on my experience of growing up in poverty, I noticed a huge difference between my experience and others who grew up in poverty. Poverty can be less traumatic and damaging if you grow up in a household that upholds Christian values. Because of my mother's faith and our church involvement, there was never any money spent on alcohol, cigarettes, lottery tickets, and countless other vices that impact families.

We were taught biblical moral standards, which were strictly upheld and avoided the damage caused by teen sex and pregnancies; my mom protected us from making the same mistakes she had. Sure, Christmas gifts were minimal; we mostly shopped at thrift stores, never had a vacation, but the rent was always paid, and there was always food on the table. All while my mom tithed from her welfare check and sent $20 monthly to World Vision for her sponsored child. In contrast, my friends who grew up in secular homes experienced teen pregnancies, drug addictions, evictions, and a host of other issues.

I was surprised to find a study that corroborated my conclusion that a Christian's experience of poverty in the US, although still filled with difficulty and shame, was less traumatic. The study found that it was evident that people of faith living in deprived neighborhoods experience better overall well-being than their non-religious neighbors living in the same area.

That's why I believe how successful we are at getting families out of poverty comes second to how successful we are at getting them to know and grow in Jesus Christ.

Debbie explained why programs like RENEW Life Center and Young*Lives* are so important. She said,

> Pregnancy centers have gotten very professional and highly organized with policies and procedures, and that's awesome, and that's necessary to a large degree, but the more we become like a counseling service where there's a distance between the people served and those serving them, the less life transformation may happen.
>
> Transformation happens when lives bump up against each other. And the most transformation I've seen

occurs in people's lives when we've crossed barriers. Our staff has gotten close to many of our Young-Lives moms, and as a result, some of them attend our churches. I had the privilege of dedicating one mom's baby to the Lord in our church!

All of a sudden, ten people from her family were up on the church platform. It was new territory for them, but we were hugging each other and celebrating life together.

The more the pregnancy center becomes like a counseling agency, the less you can invite your client over for Christmas dinner. But real change happens when people get to see life done differently.

Margaret was a client who visited our Hackensack center; she was a nanny, and if she continued with her pregnancy, it meant she risked losing her nanny position. She knew that if she chose life, she would be facing homelessness. Thankfully a teacher from a local Christian school took her into her home.

Sometimes I'd pick up Margaret and the baby's father for church; other times she attended the teacher's church; I feel her life was forever changed because people's lives got enmeshed with hers. She became a follower of Christ and a friend; someone we love and care about. She got to experience something that was a game-changer for both her and her son.

That's why I love these programs that get God's people mixed up in the lives of our moms and dads. No matter how well we serve our parents, we essentially get an hour a week with them. The rest of the time they are influenced by everybody else with different messages, financial pressures, and the stresses of life.

We only get an hour a week with them; we need to set them up for success in more lasting and tangible ways. It's like the person who becomes a Christian, and they're trying to live the Christian life, but they only spend an hour in church, with nothing outside of that all week to nurture them."

I asked Debbie, "Why is it so hard to get women to visit their local churches?"

She replied, I think one of the difficulties in getting a woman to visit a church is that she's stepping into a completely different environment, and she feels alone and out of place. But when you have these RENEW mentors and relationships, where you start becoming friends and then an invitation to church is extended, the level of trust is already there, and a mom or dad is more likely to say yes. I personally haven't seen a good result with just saying, 'Here's a list of churches, pick one.'

We want to transition these women and their partners from the pregnancy center to the church, but you need to have a bridge between them. Programs like Young-Lives and RENEW Life Center are that bridge.

Our clients' lives don't change overnight; we don't change our own lives overnight! If I want to be a better person, if I want to lose weight or start exercising every day, it takes a lot of work to turn the ship around. So why do we expect the people we serve at our center to quickly snap into a new life? It really takes getting people into their lives. We need caring Christian people, interacting with these women and men day in and day out, encouraging them, so they don't go three weeks without hope. Bringing them along to church and inviting them to women's or men's groups – things that open the door to new possibilities for them.

To that end, Lighthouse is launching a new program called *Birth of a Family*. It's a weekly program to invite the women and couples we're serving to come and learn what marriage and healthy relationships look like. We want to give them a picture of what the benefits of marriage are and give them more support in their life. RENEW is excited to support Lighthouse in this new endeavor, but we need the partnership of local Christians as well."

Debbie continued:

James 2:14-17 says, 'What good is it, my brothers and sisters if someone claims to have faith but has no deeds? Can such faith save them? Suppose a brother or a sister is without clothes and daily food. If one of you says to them, 'Go in peace; keep warm and well fed,' but does nothing about their physical needs, what good is it? In the same way, faith by itself, if it is not accompanied by action, is dead.'

A pregnancy center is about deeds and about action; the material support and the parenting support that we provide is very practical, but again, it's temporary. An organization like RENEW that really reinforces a long-term positive change in people's lives *and* that will still be in relationship with them three, four, ten, or twenty years down the road, is another tangible way of meeting physical needs. The physical needs we meet at the pregnancy center are related to the nine months of pregnancy and caring for a newborn; but who will help meet the needs of the family when the child is five and ten, and eighteen? The more we surround that family with relationships that outlast the pregnancy and the baby's first year of life, the better the outcomes we will see."

Pregnancy centers do a great job at meeting a woman in her time of crisis. They offer a compassionate ear, medically accurate information, an ultrasound to confirm pregnancy, and give her a glimpse of her baby's beating heart – plus a host of other services. The center looks for opportunities to share the gospel, and they collaborate with other partners who can help lead a mom to a local church. To use the earlier relay race term, they pass the baton to us, the Church. We provide not only the spiritual support, but also the community support that so many families desperately crave. We now get the opportunity to play a part in a mom's and baby's journey to an abundant life where they can realize their dreams. Does that excite you? I hope so.

## One Phone Call Changed Her Life

In Chapter 5, I mentioned Kerri, who, after eight years of unemployment, finally has a job and is now feeling confident and proud of herself. But that's not the whole story. Kerri was living a double life. Her children's father was very abusive. We all suspected it, but she never confirmed it. She had been living under those terrible conditions for more than 15 years.

She recently said to me, "It's like I'm two people. During the day at work, I'm in my element, and I'm feeling whole, but as I approach my house, my demeanor changes." She didn't realize that change until a coworker gave her a ride home one day and mentioned to her that she saw her countenance change as they approached her house.

Kerri didn't make much of her comment, but what her coworker Mary saw was enough for her to be concerned about Kerri. A couple of days later, Mary decided to call her at home to see how she was doing. What Mary heard going on in the background confirmed her suspicions; Kerri is living in a domestic violence situation. When Mary saw Kerri at work, she pulled her aside and said, "I'm not going to force you into anything, but what I heard going on in your house is abuse. It's not good, and it's time for you to get out."

Kerri said, "What she said impacted me; she gave it a name." Up until then, it was just life as normal for Kerri.

*Get out?* But how? And where? Could she afford an apartment on her own? Kerri had another coworker, Linda, who helped her with her budgeting. Kerri finally worked up the courage to ask

Linda if she thought she could afford an apartment independently. Linda answered no, and asked Kerri why she asked her that question.

Kerri finally broke down and told Linda everything that was happening at her house. Kerri told Linda about the violence, told her that her teenage daughter had to take medication for depression and anxiety. Kerri shared that her son was just a shell of a boy and that the toddler walked around, covering her ears. Linda, a Christian, told Kerri that she had suspected something was going on, and she had been praying for her.

Up until this point, Kerri was afraid to ask for help because she thought no one would believe her story. I could see why. I have met her partner, John. He was tall, very good looking, had a great smile, and was a charmer. But I could see right through him. She told me that he frequently made comments like, "You're lucky I'm letting you work," and "You better..., because if I leave, everything will fall apart," and "You should know how I am and be used to it." But my personal favorite was: "If you hadn't changed, I wouldn't be acting this way." That's right, John, she has changed.

That change began on a September morning when she sat in our classroom for her first day of the Getting Ahead workshop. I still remember her sad eyes. She seemed nervous and very timid, but over the next ten weeks, I saw her transform into a confident, hopeful woman. When she got a job, she took off like a rocket, and John didn't like that.

Linda asked Kerri, "Do you want to leave?" Kerri did. Linda picked up her phone and called her pastor and explained the situation. The pastor said he would have an emergency board meeting that night and get back to Linda with a response. The next day, he called, and Kerri had a home to go to with her children. The pastor's swift response was possible because his church was part of the Family Promise Network (FPN).

FPN is a network of churches that provides temporary shelter and support to working families with children who are experiencing homelessness or domestic violence. The shelter provided comes in different forms; sometimes it's space within the church, and other times it's a house or unused parsonage. This particular congregation had a house they used for missionaries on furlough as part of the Family Promise Network. God is so good.

Kerri and her children will now begin the complicated process of rebuilding their lives and healing from the trauma. She's comforted by the assurance that RENEW will be with her every step of the way. I'm grateful that Kerri and her children were rescued from their violent environment, but my heart breaks for the other women we serve, still waiting for a way out.

## Good For Her Bad For Him

Do you remember Darlene from Chapter 5? She felt pretty proud of herself, but did you know that she's also in an abusive relationship? She lives under the tyranny of her children's father. When she graduated from our Getting Ahead workshop, her dream was to get her GED.

We helped her set some goals around that, got her signed up for classes, and assigned her a mentor/tutor who would help her along. But then the fighting started because she was leaving the house too much. It got so bad that she wanted to drop her GED courses. But we suggested that if leaving the house was the problem, why not sign up for online classes? Problem solved, right? No.

Now that she's taking classes online, he hides her GED coursebook. This is petty stuff, but it exposes the truth of the matter. He wants to maintain complete control over her, and anything she does to improve herself is a threat to him. There's so much yelling, screaming, fighting, name-calling, and threatening that the children are all exhibiting stress and anxiety-related health issues.

Darlene looks at the bright side: "At least he doesn't hit me." That's not good enough, and she knows that, but she says, "It's so ingrained in you that you don't see a way out."

You might be thinking, won't a shelter solve this problem? There are two main reasons why it won't. Here's one:

In just one day in 2015, more than 31,500 adults and children fleeing domestic violence found refuge in a domestic violence emergency shelter or transitional housing program.

That same day, domestic violence programs were unable to meet more than 12,197 requests for services because of a lack of funding, staffing, or other resources. 63% (7,728) of unmet requests were for housing. Emergency shelter and transitional housing continue to be the most urgent unmet needs for domestic violence survivors.

The second reason is that shelters are not always safe places. Women who have spent time in a shelter have either been involved in or have seen physical fights break out over things like shampoo or accusations of "your kid hit my kid." Shelters do their best to prevent these types of things, but it still happens frequently. I ask myself, is this the best we can do for these moms? It's a seemingly insurmountable problem, but I know that if churches would band together around this issue we could find a solution.

I regularly check in on Darlene through text messages because her partner gets angry when he sees her talking on the phone. It's Tuesday, and I sent her a message. I want to encourage her to continue with her GED online studies, even without the book. Her text response was, "THIS WEEKEND WAS UNBEARABLE."

How am I supposed to respond to that? With "I'll pray for you?" I must have said that to her a thousand times in the last five years. I can't get myself to say that once again. I shot back an impulsive text, "Darlene, one day soon, you will be out of there, I promise."

There I go again, making a promise I have no idea how I'm going to keep. In twenty years of serving in ministry, it's only the second time I've done that. The last time God provided through His Church, I believe He'll do it again.

## The Rest Of My Story

After our third child was born, our marriage continued its downward spiral. After one very heated argument, I insisted once again that we see a marriage counselor. I told him that I refused to live like this any longer. He didn't like that at all; it enraged him, and just like that, he said he was moving out.

Overnight, my life turned upside down. He was mad that I refused to put up with his verbal abuse, and he was going to make me pay. Things went from bad to unbearably worse. I had no time for hatching a plan. A few months later, he moved out, but what I didn't know was that he stopped paying the mortgage those last few months to ensure that he would cause me maximum harm – with no regard for how his kids would be affected.

So there I was, a stay-at-home mom with three children under five, no plan, and no money. The girl who overcame generational poverty was suddenly thrown back into poverty, and the crash hit hard. I sold my jewelry to keep the lights on and buy food; I sold my house before it was foreclosed.

Before I decided to be a stay-at-home mom, I had a ten-year career in the information technology field, and I had a friend in a job placement agency specializing in IT careers. I spruced up my resumé and sent it to him. The job market was pretty bad, so it took about five months to land an entry-level position paying $40,000 a year, which was not bad considering it was 1997. I was relieved, but I didn't know the many other hardships I was about to face.

My children's father refused to give me any financial support, and because we were still legally married, I couldn't petition the court for child support. I didn't have money for a lawyer to file for a divorce; I was trapped in financial and emotional limbo. I wanted to keep my expenses to a minimum, so I decided a two-bedroom apartment would be OK. I would share a room with my daughter, and the boys would share the other room.

I quickly found out that no one would rent me a two-bedroom apartment. I needed three bedrooms, they insisted. Some landlords even made me feel embarrassed for suggesting such a thing, a lesson learned. Apparently, it's unacceptable in middle-class neighborhoods for a single mother trying to provide a safe home and great schools for her children to share a bedroom with her two-year-old daughter. Almost twenty-five years later, I still don't understand why that's such an anomaly, and it saddens me to know that the single moms we serve today are facing the same problem.

Using the rent affordability calculation of rent not going over 30-35% of your income, I knew that I would not qualify for a three-bedroom apartment. One landlord said to me, "I know I'm going to end up having to evict you in a few months." Those words stung and I felt humiliated; this went on for months. I couldn't see a way out of this Catch-22 until a friend suggested, "What if I co-sign for the apartment with you?" Thankfully, she insisted, I finally had to accept her help. Otherwise, my children and I would not have had a safe place to live.

My children and I settled into our three-bedroom apartment in the lovely town of Westfield, New Jersey. The boys started school; I had to pay for a full-day preschool for my daughter. I don't remember how much that was exactly, but I know it was a strain on my budget. I also had to hire someone to pick up my kids after school and take care of them until I got home from work at 6 p.m.; that was an additional $150 a week. I had a tight budget; I had to account for every penny.

I remember checking out at the supermarket with my four-year-old daughter. She spotted a hair detangler spray bottle that had Pocahontas on it. She wanted that bottle, she begged for it, but it was $4.95! Just a week ago, I had put back a 25¢ pack of gum because I couldn't afford it. Now she wanted this for $4.95. Looking at her face, I didn't want to say no. I wanted her to be happy.

I bought the detangler and decided I had to figure out how to make up for it in my budget. By the way, she thought the detangler lasted for months because I secretly kept refilling the bottle with water. Twenty-two years later I still have that bottle. It's a reminder of that challenging time in my life.

Those years were painful. It's by the grace of God that I made it through. It took almost two years to receive regular child support. My ex-husband fought me tooth and nail, but it made a huge difference. It was the difference between making my kids a real dinner and pretending to be the cool parent who gave them breakfast for dinner. For me, the most troubling thing about my story and the reason I share it, is that as bad as that experience was, I had it "good." I had a skill set to fall back on, colleagues in the industry to help me get a job, a friend who took a risk by co-signing a lease and eventually receiving the child support due to my children. The women we serve at RENEW have none of that going for them.

I remember one particular day early in our separation, everything felt out of control. I kept a stiff upper lip throughout the day for the sake of my children, but after I put them to bed, I threw myself on my bedroom floor and cried out to the Lord. "God, I'm no longer asking you for help; help is not enough anymore. I need a miracle." That's exactly what He gave me – miracles, miracles in the form of people He sent to provide the support I needed to get through that difficult time. The moms we serve are praying for miracles too. Could that be you?

## It's Your Turn to Choose

I have talked about the choices women and men have to make when faced with a crisis pregnancy. I have talked about some of the difficult choices they have to make afterwards. Now it's your turn to make some choices; you chose to read this book, so you have already made one good one. I encourage you to make at least one more. Here are a few suggestions:

- Connect with your local pregnancy center and other pro-life support ministries like RENEW Life Center. Take a tour and learn more about what they do to save and transform lives every day; find out how you can volunteer or donate to support their life-affirming work.

- Be that person who is the answer to prayer for one of our moms. Just two hours a week of your time can change the course of a mom's life when you make a regular mentorship/discipleship commitment.

- Let's not forget about the men; husbands and single men are needed as godly role models and mentors to the fathers we serve.

- Become a church liaison; share our ministry opportunities with your church for funding support and program partnerships.

- Share your gifts and talents with us. There are many non-client contact volunteer roles to be filled, this behind-the-scenes work makes a huge impact on the face of the ministry.

I could go on with this list, the needs are many, and I believe the Church is the answer to meeting those needs. If you have made it to the end of this book, you are probably a church member! My prayer is that you're not overwhelmed by the great and ongoing needs in the lives and stories shared here, but that you are inspired to become a part of the great work God is doing in pro-life ministry.

The Apostle Paul compares the Christian life to a race, and he challenges us to run in such a way as to win the prize. I compare pro-life ministry to a relay race where everyone wins, mom, dad, baby, and for certain, you will, too. Remember, you don't have to be an expert, and you don't have to do it all; you only have to be ready and willing to open your heart and extend your hand to grab the baton.

# Bibliography

National Network to End Domestic Violence, "Domestic Violence Counts 2015-A 24-hour census of domestic violence shelters and services" https://nnedv.org/mdocs-posts/census_2015_handout_national-summary

Office of Disease Prevention and Health Promotion, "2020 Topics and Objectives: Early and Middle Childhood", https://www.healthypeople.gov/2020/topics-objectives/topic/early-and-middle-childhood

Psychiatric Times, "Addressing Poverty and Mental Illness", https://www.psychiatrictimes.com/view/addressing-poverty-and-mental-illness

Kevin M. Simon, MD , Michaela Beder, MD , Marc W. Manseau, MD, MPH - June 29, 2018 - Volume 35, Issue 6

# Appendix

Bridges out of Poverty: Strategies for Professionals and Communities, Philip E. DeVol, Ruby K. Payne

Generous Justice, Timothy Keller

Getting AHEAD in a Just-Gettin'-By World, Philip E. DeVol

What Every Church Member Should Know About Poverty, Bill Ehlig and Ruby K. Payne

When Helping Hurts, Steve Corbett & Brian Fikkert

# About The Author

Marisol has served in pregnancy resource center ministries for 20 years, first as a volunteer, and then as the director of an urban center. Her years of experience in serving women facing unplanned pregnancies led her to see the many needs and obstacles women in poverty were facing. Burdened by the struggles that confronted these new moms, Marisol co-founded RENEW Life Center in 2013, to fill the gap that exists after the services offered at a pregnancy center end.

Marisol is the recipient of the following awards:

The Andy Anderson Award For Outstanding Volunteer Service

The Markee "D" Ministries Supporter of the Year Award

Certificate of Special Congressional Recognition (for outstanding and invaluable service to the community)

Certificate of Recognition from The Office of the Passaic County Clerk (For outstanding contribution towards the Paterson Partners for Life Center in helping families thrive)

The Power of One Life Award (In honor of her generous stewardship of time, talents and treasure to save and change lives)

Arise NJ Outstanding Citizen Award (for helping families overcome poverty)

Before becoming the co-founder and Executive Director of RENEW Life Center, Marisol worked for Gateway Pregnancy Center, LIFENET, and the New Jersey Family Policy Council. She also previously worked in the Information Technology field with corporations such as Verizon Wireless and Prudential.

## Volunteer Roles

Commissioner on the NJ Human Trafficking Commission
Paterson Alliance Board of Trustees
Life Education Council Board of Trustees
Living Free of New Jersey, Board of Trustees

# RENEW
## life center

Breaking the cycle of generational poverty to
Move Families from **Surviving to Thriving**

---

 **@RENEWLifeCenterNJ** • **@renew_lifenj**

RENEW equips single moms who have chosen life to overcome
generational poverty. Our educational programs, mentoring, and
leadership development transform lives and lead to economic
self-sufficiency, healthy relationships, and restored dignity.

To inquire about volunteering or other
partnership opportunities, please email
**info@RENEWLifeCenterNJ.org** or call
**862.257.3817** or visit **RENEWLifeCenterNJ.org**

Childcare volunteers,
mentors and facilitators
are needed for *Getting
Ahead* classes.

"Since graduating I have accomplished
so much! One of the things I am most
proud of is that after being unemployed
for eight years, I finally have a job I
love! I went from not having any
confidence and feeling like my life was
out of control to now walking with my
head held high. Even more exciting is
that I can pass on all I have learned to
my children so they will have a leg up
starting off their lives. There is no other
way to say it but that RENEW and the
Getting Ahead workshop was life
changing for me and my children!"

- Getting Ahead Graduate

Looking to bring or expand
on this topic at your
pro-life ministry or church?

# BOOK MARISOL

to speak at your next conference or
church event

Also available for TV, Radio, and Podcast
Interviews

---

Contact us at:
info@RENEWLifeCenterNJ.org
862-257-3817
www.RENEWLifeCenterNJ.org

Made in the USA
Middletown, DE
28 April 2021